INSPIRED BY PARIS

Why Borrowing from the French Is Better Than Being French

JORDAN PHILLIPS

Inspired by Paris: Why Borrowing from the French Is Better Than Being French

Every possible effort has been made to ensure that the information contained in this book is accurate at the time it goes to press. No responsibility for loss or damage as a result of the material in this book can be accepted by the author or publisher.

Copyright © 2016 Jordan Phillips

Illustrations by Angeline Melin, www.angelinemelin.com, 2016.
Back cover photograph by Goncalo Silva, 2015.

First edition 2016
ISBN-10: 0692699295
ISBN-13: 9780692699294
Library of Congress Control Number: 2016907167
Lure of Luxe LLC, New York, NY

This book is dedicated to my fellow Francophiles,
because Paris is always a good idea...
whether in reality or just fantasy.

CONTENTS

Introduction

nstagram Paris is the stuff that dreams are made of. It's all marriage proposals along the banks of the Seine, stacks of pristine pastel macarons dusted in gold leaf, and cobblestone alleyways filled with quaint little bistros and boutiques. It's those manicured trees that stand symmetrically at attention like obedient soldiers, boasting bright greens and then oranges and yellows until they succumb to winter's defeat. But the real Paris—though undeniably beautiful—is often gray and unfriendly. Simple tasks are made to be unnecessarily complicated, the word of the day is always *non*, and complaining is a national sport. Then again, as with anything intense and appealing, one can't help but go back for more.

Highs and lows are an inevitable part of all irresistible relationships. The things that once attracted you to a boyfriend (he's mysterious) have another side that eventually wears you down (he's fucking crazy). Either you realize this, decide that you too are flawed, and enjoy the good parts and just deal with the disappointing ones—or you move on. Paris has this same sort of palpable grip on me, constantly pulling me close and then pushing me away.

If you frequently fantasize about traveling to France, then I think you'll enjoy our little journey together. It doesn't matter if you're headed to Paris next week or if you never make it there at all. Through my love affair with all things French, I've learned that—as in so many things in life—often fantasy is better than reality. But we'll get into that later.

The silence of the suburbs has always felt suffocating to me. Some people find comfort in green pastures; I find comfort in walking through a crowded city while music flows through my headphones, dictating my stride. Dancing in a sea of people, or even riding the subway, provides some sort of "we're all in this together" reassurance that I crave. The din of a busy café—the clinking of glasses, the repeated clattering of forks and knives onto porcelain, the ebb and flow of small talk, the raucous laughter, and the hushed conversations—provides pure joy.

And the best din of all can be found in a Parisian café. While you try to identify all of the various languages floating about, you watch people fondle the same *tasse* of espresso for what seems like an eternity, and you hear the satisfying swoosh of wine bottles being opened, even at lunch. You see the specials drawn on chalkboards in precise cursive letters, really simple dishes that sound so much more sophisticated just because they're written in French. Would you rather have *poulet* or chicken? *Moi, je prends le poulet,* thank you very much.

Picture those woven rattan chairs found outside every bistro and brasserie. Okay, so they're not especially comfortable, and they leave those unsightly crosshatch marks across the backs of our legs, but they're reassuringly charming. One look, and you're instantly transported to a terrace in France. That's a powerful thing for some simple sidewalk furniture to provide. Put a picture of a French café table and two chairs on Pinterest, and it will be pinned and repinned indefinitely. You don't see people plastering diner booths all over social media with that emoji with hearts for eyes. Why? Because one represents speed, efficiency, and mediocre food; the other represents lingering for hours, people-watching, and perhaps engaging in a little romance. You don't see a wobbly little metal table and two uncomfortable chairs. You see possibilities, fantasies, and adventure. You see life, waiting to be lived.

Chapter 1

. . . .

An American in Paris

I love French men and French culture and French wine and French architecture and French food, along with a lot of other French things. Show me a wedge of oozy cheese or a slightly dilapidated Mansard roof, and I still swoon, no matter how many I see.

You'll notice I didn't mention French women. They can be total bitches. But I appreciate them too.

I'm a bona fide Jean-Luc Godard–idolizing, striped-shirt-wearing, sparkling Eiffel Tower–loving Francophile. I love the clichés, and I love most of the things that I discovered once I learned about more than just the clichés.

It all began when I arrived in France for the first time on a family vacation, awoken from a comatose stupor by my parents at the Nice airport. For a girl used to the occasional Hawaiian vacation, jet lag was confusing and consuming. I was young and naïve. It was my first experience with sleep deprivation, long before all-nighters for studying, partying, loving, fighting, working, worrying, or comforting a crying newborn. At the time, the feeling of having to stay awake despite every inch of my mind and body fighting me was entirely new. I have no idea how my parents got my little sister and me into the back of that taxi, given our heavy eyelids and noodle-like bodies, but somehow they did.

And then I opened my eyes.

Having been born in Texas and raised in California, where everything that's nice is new and bigger is always better, I underestimated how utterly different it would feel to be in a place where peeling paint and cramped quarters could actually seem appealing. The flawless architecture looked like it was plucked straight from those vintage French Riviera travel posters, though the distinct lack of upkeep was at first jarring to my American eyes. But I quickly began to appreciate how a little decay softened the façades and added to the overall charm. Far, far away from the land of lawns and SUVs and strip malls, I marveled at the ground floors of the apartment buildings, containing *boulangeries* and *fromageries* and *boucheries*. When I looked above the ground floors, I saw the apartments themselves, and I vowed to live just like that one day.

Everything was different. I stared out the car window and intently watched people at the stoplights, absorbing every detail that I could. French kids my age looked so much cooler, I thought as I glanced down at my Abercrombie jeans and bulky white sneakers. (Little did I know that French people would later stand in ridiculously long lines to shop at Abercrombie & Fitch—a phenomenon that I still do not understand—and that all *parisiens* and *parisiennes* would be wearing jeans with bright-white Stan Smiths.)

Even the billboards were different. A man with longish hair and a five-o'clock shadow tried to sell me coffee. Then a scantily clad woman offered up anticellulite cream. Next another man with longish hair and a five-o'clock shadow frolicked with a scantily clad woman as they peered down on me, enticing me to try the latest perfume. This was before the widespread use of sex-sells advertising in the United States (Marky Mark having shocked the nation by dropping his pants for Calvin Klein only a few years earlier), so the in-your-face sensuality of the French ads made my eyes pop. I loved it.

A radio announcer enthusiastically shouted through the stereo between songs, speaking in a language that I so badly wanted to understand but couldn't. The *nst nst* of the then-foreign Euro dance music, so different from West Coast grunge and hip-hop, vibrated throughout the car, furthering the trancelike feeling that it was all a dream. The smooth ride of the French taxi—a gorgeous gray Mercedes—was a welcome surprise for someone used to the unnecessary bumpiness of shoddy American taxis.

Within five minutes flat, I fell hard for the sheer foreignness of it all. Life would never be the same. I would never be the same. It was as if the clouds parted and the universe opened itself up to me, revealing that I actually knew nothing about the world but that I had an entire lifetime to explore it.

When we reached our hotel, the bellhop threw open the double doors in our room, bathing us in bright Riviera sunlight. Our room was one big explosion of floral prints, not in the dowdy Laura Ashley way that my mother favored but in a much more dignified way (sorry, Mom). I plopped down onto the bed, turned my face toward the sun, and smiled. Just before dozing off to sleep, I took a closer look at the cracked but elegant double doors with their ornate handles. So chic, I thought, and so unlike our efficient but styleless ones back home.

Those doors sum up a lot about France: so chic but wildly impractical. Inefficiency is one of the worst qualities about France and simultaneously one of its best. American big business, with its emphasis on the bottom line and the relentless pursuit of lowering costs, is all about efficiency. Consumers find this comforting in the short term (things are cheaper, faster, and cleaner) but not always so great in the long term (things are of lower quality, aren't good for us, and are totally destroying the planet). Practically everything charming about France would be ruined by Americans, despite our best intentions.

If I took over a *boulangerie,* for example, I would start patching the cracks in the walls and marketing the place like crazy. We can't help it; it's the American way. A French person wouldn't notice the cracks in the walls in the first place and would think the bread should speak for itself, which is either poetic or frustrating, depending on your point of view.

Paris is the most beautiful city in the world. I'm biased, but I've never come across anyone who refutes this. It just is. Once when I was standing in front of the *préfecture de police* in Paris, an American woman approached me and asked me if it was the Louvre. Let me repeat that: she thought that the police station was the Louvre museum. That's how inherently beautiful Paris is (and, yes, how inherently ignorant some Americans can be). I love New York and all of its glory, but I can assure you that no one confuses a police station with the Met. And don't even get me started about nighttime in the City of Light, when *la Tour Eiffel* sparkles on the hour every hour for five minutes beginning at nightfall. I don't care what the real Parisians say. It's just magical.

Three subsequent trips solidified my undying love for France; two were in reality and the other just a fantasy. Luckily, I had kept a detailed journal from those two weeks in the South of France with my family as a teenager, and I got to reread it before my next trip. In it, I had written this:

And sitting at one of the little outside French cafes (like in the movie *Sabrina*), I realized that I *have* to come back here alone. I could sit for hours and just soak up the inspiration. Now I know why artists, writers, poets, and designers come here. Just being in this atmosphere makes me want to read, write, draw, and cook.

About a decade later, I did just that and went to Paris by myself. When you travel alone with an open mind, the possibilities are limitless. My trip lasted only a week, but so many crazy moments were packed in that it still provides the ultimate mental highlight reel.

I met friends, and I met a few guys who became more than friends. I met chefs, I met artists, and I even met a girl who lived in my hometown. I drank countless *coupes* of Champagne every evening and then counteracted the Champagne by devouring several perfect, buttery, flaky croissants every morning. I conquered the Musée d'Orsay and the Pompidou, and I swapped stories in bistros with newly made friends.

Then there was Jean-Paul. On my last night in Paris, I strolled down Rue du Faubourg Saint-Honoré, lost in my mental oohing and aahing over every single architectural detail, when, like a mirage, a dark-haired Frenchman—complete with five-o'clock shadow—pulled up in a car beside me and rolled down his window. We engaged in a verbal tug-of-war for at least five minutes, him insisting that I must join him immediately for dinner, me shyly insisting that I shouldn't, but, as I learned later, Frenchmen really do not take no for an answer. (Warning: they can also be extremely emotional.) I caved and jumped in.

The thrill of whizzing through the streets of Paris quickly whisked away any sensible doubts about getting into cars with strange men in foreign countries at night by myself. We met up with his friend, who turned out to be a stylish woman in her forties wearing white jeans and gold Hermès bracelets that jangled as she gestured. Over dinner at a little Italian restaurant, she talked about her husband and children, and Jean-Paul recounted recent travels. I was on my best behavior—with my fork in my left hand, tines down, and my knife in my right—as I pretended to be a sophisticated grown-up, hoping they wouldn't notice that I definitely did not fit in.

After dinner came one fantastic scene after another, Paris serving as our backdrop, like a movie montage out of my dreams. When we'd finished at the clubs, we went back to the Parisienne's place, where her boyfriend was waiting. We danced; we laughed; we drank. When the conversation turned back to French, I wandered around and allowed my eyes to take in every detail of her apartment. Vintage African rugs covered elegantly battered oak floors, allowing just the right amount of chevron zigs and zags to peek out around the edges. Colorful modern-art pieces toned down the ornate wood paneling in the sitting room, while black-and-white photographs haphazardly lined the walls of the hallway, making the sparkling crystal chandelier at the end seem like an afterthought and not the main attraction. The apartment was clean but cluttered, containing layers upon layers of a life well lived. To this day, the memory of her apartment inspires me.

Back in the sitting room, surrounded by pictures of the husband and children—who were out of town—I chatted with her boyfriend and marveled at the fact that nobody seemed shocked by this arrangement in the slightest. It wasn't even something to hide.

We danced, we drank, and we laughed some more.

A decade earlier, I had written in my travel journal, "I felt like a playful child and an experienced, worldly adult in one. It was an experience I'll never forget."

Apparently, in France, some things never change.

Back at Jean-Paul's apartment later, I got a private tour of an aesthetic that was completely the opposite but equally chic. Clean and modern, it looked like something straight out of *Architectural Digest.*

Whereas the Parisienne's apartment was warm and colorful, Jean-Paul's was sleek and gray. I remember running my fingers over the cold, thick concrete countertop in the kitchen and later enjoying the rain shower with wall-to-wall glass.

For whatever reason, he became obsessed with the idea of me moving there. He mentioned marriage. Seriously? We'd just met. It was tempting for all of about two seconds—the two seconds stemming from the fact that the public relations firm I worked for had an office in Paris, and technically I could transfer. For all of his qualities (namely French, right time, right place, to-die-for apartment), he was just not at all my type.

Hours later, still in my dress from the night before, or really from the night that never ended, I raced over to Saint-Germain-des-Prés for an espresso and one last croissant before catching my flight to California. I wasn't ready to leave. In one of my cheesiest moments to date, I actually twirled on the Pont des Arts with a huge smile plastered across my face. And then I twirled some more. Life was good. I had fantasized about possibilities and adventure, and Paris delivered in spades.

My next trip to Paris would not involve any condoms. It was my honeymoon. Unfortunately, Jason didn't take to the city at first, and he seemed downright uncomfortable. I got it. Rude waiters and mysterious animal parts weren't for everyone, but could I be married to a man who didn't love Paris? It was unfathomable. Luckily, after a twenty-four-hour adjustment period, he fell in love with it too, so much so that later we ended up living there for two years at his suggestion. We took romantic walks in the rain, tucked into brasseries, and warmed up with piping hot bowls of *cassoulet*. Drunk in love and drunk on great French wine, we strolled along the Seine arm in arm each night.

The day after we returned from our honeymoon, I found out that I was pregnant.

You really don't need a passport for a trip to Paris—or anywhere else, for that matter. You can travel in your heart, your head, and your stomach, which sums up my third "trip" to Paris. While pregnant, I made everything from Ina Garten's *Barefoot in Paris: Easy French Food You Can Make at Home*, humming along to Vanessa Paradis while I cooked and baked for hours every evening. What pregnant woman doesn't want to eat a *croque monsieur?* It's a ham-and-cheese sandwich on white bread dripping with melted cheese and butter. Later, while on partial bed rest, I whisked myself away from my temporarily terribly boring existence by imagining bistros, baguettes, and those adorable wrought-iron *balcons.*

When it came time to pack a bag for the hospital before I had my daughter, I read every baby book that I could get my hands on, one of which recommended packing a picture of my "happy place" to transport me away when labor got intense. (That obviously turned out to be a load of crap, because the only way to be transported to a happy place in this situation is via epidural.) I am embarrassed to admit that not only did I follow that book's silly advice but I also packed a little framed black-and-white picture of Paris. It was my happy place, and it still is.

Your embracing of other cultures doesn't need to be as extreme as mine. You can gain so much just by reading, listening to music, cooking, drinking, and exploring your culture of choice on social media. No matter where you live, you can learn about Argentina by taking tango lessons and searching for the perfect malbec. You don't necessarily need to go to Buenos Aires to discover your sultry Latin side. Vacations are short; expanding your horizons through learning brings lifelong enjoyment.

I think this "traveling of the mind" concept might be harder for Americans to embrace than for other cultures because many of us tend to be very to-the-point, driven by results, and generally somewhat Machiavellian. We also love a good fairy tale, and Hollywood provides us plenty of ammo to fuel our fantasies. In the American version of a story, the fantasy is almost always fulfilled. So learning about another culture for no real reason or contemplating travel without plans to actually leave the house might feel a bit odd.

Some researchers from the Netherlands took it upon themselves to do a psychological study about the connection between antici- pation and happiness. The study, published in *Applied Research in Quality of Life* in 2010, found that vacationers felt happiest before their trips.[1] By removing the end result, you free yourself to just enjoy the journey. As the saying goes, "anticipation is the greater part of pleasure."[2]

If you haven't already, start watching French films, and you'll realize that they don't feel the need to wrap up everything with a pretty Hollywood bow at the end. Sometimes they do; sometimes they don't. *Ça dépend.* French films don't need to have a happy end- ing or even an ending at all. Travel is the same; you can save, plan, anticipate, and complete a trip to Paris, or you can just be inspired by Paris. Either way, if you go about it with an open mind and a desire to learn, you will not be disappointed.

Chapter 2

....

La Vie Est Belle

Ah, the Parisienne. This much-discussed species of woman has been dazzling and perplexing the rest of us for centuries. She's a good girl, she's a bad girl, and she is most definitely cool and aloof. She pretends that she doesn't put much thought into how she appears to others, but she absolutely does. Aristocratic French women perfected the *déshabillé* look (seemingly carelessly dressed while actually being on-trend and fashionable) in the eighteenth century, and it has trickled down ever since. Though Parisian style might come across as effortless and a bit badass, there are rules. Many, many rules.

As New Yorker Marina Khorosh wrote in *Vogue* about her years living in Paris,

> Don't speak too loudly, don't let your outfit speak for you, don't leave the house in sweatpants, always say "bonjour!" Living here

is like being at your grandmother's house, if your grandmother happens to reside in an antiquated mansion: exquisite yet—dare I say it?—exceedingly boring…Unlike in Paris, where you dread the once-over stares, in New York you come to enjoy them, as they most likely convey admiration, or at least begrudging respect for doing your own thing.[3]

Shortly after moving to Paris, I started dressing up to avoid the disapproving looks of the *grandes dames* in my apartment building. I stopped wearing workout clothes to the yoga class right down the street because everyone else looked chic going in and out. I ditched my California-girl sandals and ripped jeans and T-shirts. I love fashion and adore dressing up, so it's not that it was a burden—I enjoyed it—but in hindsight it was a problem because I started doing it for them and not for me.

Parisiennes under age forty don't really wear makeup, and they go with "roll out of bed" hair, which is the opposite of my routine. I'm all about putting on a good face and whipping out the curling iron. Contrary to my nature, I went through a phase in which I wore barely any makeup, with the exception of a bright-red lip for nighttime, because that's what the Parisiennes did, and I wanted to be one. But I look like crap without makeup. And red lipstick just makes my red splotchy bits look even redder and splotchier. I felt ugly and self-conscious. I felt like I was disappearing.

But I fit in!

One day I went to get a trim from my ridiculously cool hair stylist, and she cut it almost all off, making it an exact copy of her supershort hair.

She said, "There, now you look more French."

Bitch.

It was seriously half an inch long in the back. Think Gwyneth circa *Sliding Doors*. But I don't look like Gwyneth, and I still didn't look

French, and my husband hated it. I cried. I felt awful and did not look like myself, but I cannot even tell you how many compliments I received from French women, which is practically a needle-in-a-haystack situation and therefore something that makes you pay attention.

It was all my fault. I got so caught up in trying to be something that I wasn't that I lost myself in the process. The reasons are clear, and I'll spare you the unpleasant details, but they were pretty much the usual suspects of daddy issues, low self-esteem, and a youth spent in a fairly boring town from which I longed to escape.

But I'm okay with my failed experiments. Call me superficial, call me desperate, but at least I'm open to trying new things, no matter how ridiculous they are. When we surround ourselves with the same friends and the same routines, we aren't really living. What is life like for someone who doesn't emulate others and who rejects them instead? Never mind. I really don't want to peek into that overly confident headspace. Because to yearn and to learn leads to freedom from monotony.

Playing it safe is boring. Playing it safe is for the Parisians.

Living in Paris was the best experience that I've ever had because it changed me for the better in more ways than I can possibly explain. It is a breathtakingly beautiful city with unforgettable moments and life lessons aplenty. But, just like in relationships, once the mystery was gone, Paris's moodiness became a bit oppressive. It was time to break up. I love you, but let's just be friends. With benefits.

I thought back to the quintessentially French wrought-iron balconies that I had often daydreamed of before moving there. My apartment had an exquisite *balcon*; in two years, I had sat out there only once. A rare sunny day in Paris, amid all of the countless gray ones, called for escaping to a café terrace, not sitting in cramped quarters overlooking traffic. The dream of it meant more to me than the reality. It made for some great photos though.

Once we moved back to the United States and got settled in New York (which took all of about one week thanks to the hyperefficient twenty-four-hour on-demand delivery of anything! Anytime! Anywhere!), I don't think we ate French food for nine months. We could not get away fast enough from the memory of senseless bureaucracy, the frustration of how long it took to complete basic day-to-day tasks, and the classic expat sentiment of feeling like tourists in our own city.

But then, like a rebirth of sorts, we went right back to our Francophile ways. Paris has a way of wooing you back. The moody boyfriend wasn't that crazy, was he? And so good looking.

In the years since, I've fallen somewhat into the French community, between my involvement with the French Institute Alliance Française and my daughter's with the Lycée Français de New York. I'm raising the least-American American child, one who speaks French *sans accent.* Often I still feel like an American in Paris.

I have over the years unwound all of the "French-ifying" of my look. My hair is long and bright blond, and I wear as much makeup as I damn well please. Some days I dress up and go all out, and some days I wear ratty vintage T-shirts and frayed jeans. And sometimes I even wear (gasp!) flip-flops. When certain French women deliver their overtly backhanded compliments, I simply smile and sweetly say thank you because I finally—*finally*—don't care what they think. I don't want to look like them anymore. I just want to look like me.

The great thing about being surrounded by Parisiennes is that they most likely will never approve of or admire you, so eventually you are forced to surrender and stop caring what they think. I call it wisdom through rejection. French women—and people in general—are going to judge you no matter what, so you might as well do whatever you want.

The path to shallow enlightenment can be yours, my friend. Find your look and own it, and I'll bet you that more than just your outward appearance will shift. That could even mean not putting much thought into how you look and instead focusing on other things. Whatever floats your boat. We all have different values, priorities, desires, and constraints when it comes to how we put ourselves together. Do what makes you happy; do what makes you *you.*

I frequently used to refer to myself as a Californian, because that's where I was raised and what I thought shaped me the most. But a wise Frenchman corrected me and pointed out that we are the sum of all of our experiences and thus cannot firmly say that we are this or we are that. I brushed it off in the moment but then headed to California a couple of weeks later for a family vacation, and you know what? He was right. I'm no longer a Californian; I'm someone who grew up in California, which is a subtle but important difference.

We now live in one big melting pot, where it's much easier than in the past to embrace all parts of ourselves. "Society" and "culture" are loaded terms, because so much of them are about doing things to fit in with others. But if we care too much about what others think, we don't allow ourselves to fully embrace all that life has to offer.

Everyone is beautiful in her own way. The standards of beauty finally seem to be changing, which I believe is in part due to social media. In a stark contrast from the past, when the standards of beauty were in the hands of a few advertising executives and magazine editors, we are now exposed to selfies from a variety of body types and skin tones. Now we as an international society set the bar for what is beautiful. We don't have to look like French girls—or anyone else, for that matter.

But we can learn from them. Parisiennes don't skimp on the quality or application of good body lotions, rich eye creams, or seductive perfumes, but they wear very minimal makeup (if any), especially during the daytime. Hair does not need to be washed every day, or every other day, or every third day, and it doesn't need to be styled or even brushed. If you are looking to save time and money, you should certainly study the Parisienne's beauty routine.

Personally, I've taken the body lotion/eye cream/perfume part and ditched the rest. I'm a "more is more" kind of girl, and frankly I find moderation to be quite dull. But everyone is different, and this type of approach to beauty is perfect for girls who are low maintenance but still want to have that *je ne sais quoi.*

Either way, it's better to just be yourself. The French way of coolness often comes at the expense of individuality and acceptance of others. Many Parisians seem to have a total incapacity to accept another way of dressing or grooming; I think that a tolerant and dynamic society is preferable. Throughout history, many remarkable beauties and style icons maintained their own styles, and they embraced what others considered flaws. Figure out what suits you, have fun, and go at it with confidence.

Chapter 3

....

Faux Real

French people are not snobby, but Parisians sure can be. Paris is Paris; the rest of France is "not Paris." You can move to New York or LA or San Francisco and have a close group of friends within a relatively short amount of time, but this is not the case with Parisians. Where you went to school and who you went to school with and who your parents are—or aren't—mean something. They mean a lot, actually. *Liberté, égalité, fraternité— oui!*—but only within your very specific social class. Some would describe Parisian society as impenetrable.

In general, Americans think new acquaintances are innocent until proven guilty, whereas French people tend to think the opposite. Where we see opportunities to meet new people, they see threats. Or often they just don't see us at all.

As Olivier Magny writes in *Stuff Parisians Like: Discovering the Quoi in the Je Ne Sais Quoi,*

By the age of twenty-three, Parisians have found all of their friends for life. Parisians have three groups of friends: child-hood friends, friends from high school, and friends from college. Add a handful of friends they met on vacations and the one or two remaining from the countless hours they spent as kids at sports or music practice and you'll have it all...Newcomers to Paris can therefore only befriend Parisians of age twenty-three and under. If aiming older, only *provinciaux* and foreigners will be available. The only way to make Parisian friends is to start a relationship with a person that has befriended Parisians when they were younger than twenty-three. This will grant you the honor of their company. When entering this prestigious circle, you will be a disruptive element in a group that has most likely been static for several years. This will be the source of much jealousy, drama, and talking. Excessive friendliness will be considered obscene flirtation. Be prepared to be hated by people of your gender or loved by people from the other.[4]

The number one thing I hear French women make fun of Americans for is our penchant for incessantly complimenting others about their clothing and appearances.

"Oh my gawd! Your earrings are amazing!" says the American woman as the French woman recoils.

I can see why this habit is viewed as fake, especially because the compliment might not seem genuine (and sometimes it is not). But the point of the compliment is not the authenticity of the words themselves; the point of the compliment is to make the other person feel good. And—FYI, Frenchies—trying to make people feel good about themselves is an honorably genuine pursuit in itself.

Unbeknownst to the French, this verbal olive branch (a) fills the often awkward silence between strangers and acquaintances, (b) sets a positive tone and shows the other person that you do not bite, and

(c) gives you immediate clues to her personality—how she responds and whether or not she compliments you back speak volumes. So this seemingly silly comment actually accomplishes quite a bit in just a few seconds.

I also often hear French women claim that while they are hard to get to know in the beginning, once you do break through, you will be close for life; meanwhile, they say that Americans are nice to everyone from the beginning but that these niceties are not necessarily real or lasting. And cue cultural clashes. A French woman assumes that an American being sweet to her means that she'd like to begin a friendship, when really, the American is just being polite and dipping her toe in the water. An American assumes that a Parisienne being cold and distant means she's not interested, when really, this is just the normal Parisian procedure among strangers. Misunderstandings are inevitable.

American women are generally quite warm and friendly to other women they don't know, whether in public restrooms or at parties. They believe in being nice until someone gives them a reason to be otherwise. They'll say hi and flash a smile, throw in a compliment about your shoes, and see where it goes. It doesn't necessarily need to go anywhere. You might never speak to each other again, or you might end up becoming BFFs. It's all part of the process of filtering new people in and out of our lives in a manner that more or less preserves others' feelings.

Two American women can be kind toward each other—clothing compliments ablaze—for years or decades without them ever becoming at all close or hanging out together. A French woman posing as a fly on the wall would view this as fake, but it just means that the two women are not meant to be friends and are being polite because they run into each other often. Somewhere early on, one or both of the women realized that they aren't compatible, so they created a certain distance. They never got past the superficial compliments and small-talk stage, but that does not mean they need to ignore or snub each other. American women can be friendly without being friends. This is not fake; it's civilized.

Meanwhile, a Parisienne needs to see another woman over and over again on numerous occasions before showing warmth. She will not necessarily smile—or sometimes even acknowledge the other woman in any way—until she feels certain that they have plenty of acquaintances in common and that it is safe to proceed.

If a Parisienne attends a party filled with only American people that she does not know, she can have a great time and leave the party feeling pretty good about herself. She might have several lengthy conversations—albeit somewhat meaningless ones—and she might think that she has made several new friends. She may then be surprised to find out that the Americans were just being nice and had no intention of following up, and she may feel confused because what she perceived as progress was not indeed "real."

If an American attends a party filled with only Parisians that she does not know, she's screwed. I'll bet you anything that she leaves the party feeling unwelcome and insecure. In order to become friends with them, she'd have to go back again and again and endure the same torture until she broke through. But after all of this blatant rejection, an American might not want to hang out with these people, so she will withdraw herself and will probably come across as fake because she's terrified of showing her thoughts and feelings after such initial cold treatment. It's an unfortunate cycle.

The ideal approach would be a little of both: American openness and warmth with some French candor. Why not be nice when meeting new people but perhaps discuss deeper subjects right off the bat? That way everyone feels welcomed, and it's clear from the beginning who has real friend potential.

So which party would you rather attend?

The American party would definitely be easier. And you could be as loud as you wanted. And the music would be much better. However, the problem with the American path to friendship is that it does take quite some time before any subjects that truly matter are discussed. Talking about politics, religion, and sexuality at dinners or parties is generally a big no-no for Americans, which is such a shame because those are the most interesting things to talk about.

Meanwhile, French people are all for deliberating over these topics—even with strangers—and they view a disagreement as normal banter, not as offensive. As the extremely quotable Michel de Montaigne (basically the inventor of the personal essay) put it, "There is no conversation more boring than the one where everybody agrees." The total separation of church and state during the Third Republic set the tone for the conversational liberation now enjoyed at dinner parties across France. It's never dull. As the outpour of support following the Charlie Hebdo shootings shows, lack of censorship is of the utmost importance. Citizens of France can, and do, question everything.

This is the part that's won me over and that captivates me enough to keep diving into the Parisienne-infested waters, though obviously after setting up a strong emotional cage for protection. I highly value secularism and freedom of speech, and I love a good debate. As it turns out, I would rather attend both parties.

Angéline Mélin

Chapter 4

La Joie de Vivre

When I was a child, I longed to be a teen, and when I became a teen, I longed to be an adult (of legal drinking age, of course). Once I turned twenty-one, I focused on career goals. After I checked off those goals on my life's to-do list, I focused on personal goals (getting married, becoming a mother). But here's the thing about American-style life goals: once you achieve them, then what?

In France, these high-pressure, age-specific goals don't really exist. Because of the lack of flexibility employers have in hiring and firing, the economy, and the nature of work contracts, French university graduates often spend years searching for full-time, long-term, decent-paying jobs with benefits. It is not uncommon for graduates to do years of internships and short-term projects, so there's really no set time in which one is expected to have a "real" job. Making lots of money is not considered to be a high priority and is sometimes discouraged completely.

In addition, marriage isn't a goal for many French women, and it is certainly not a prerequisite for having children. It is not rare—or frowned upon—for French couples to live together for decades, have children, and never get married. Flashy diamond engagement rings and bridal showers aren't a thing, nor are dreams of blow-the-budget white gowns and lavish wedding receptions. Marriage ceremonies are conducted at the town hall and are often celebrated simply with a small group of friends and family.

Meanwhile, American girls grow up with a lot of pressure, excitement, and expectations around milestones that have turned into highly commercialized events. Somewhere between the Barbie dolls and reality shows, many of us are trained to aspire to the following:

- Once you find a serious boyfriend, start researching diamond cuts, because your new goal is to get engaged.

- Once you get a job, strive for a better title and more money.

- Once you are engaged, rope your friends into spending a ton of money on gifts and outfits for your engagement party, bridal shower, and bachelorette party, and then dwell on every little detail of the wedding of your dreams.

- Once you are married, find and buy your first home, even if you can't afford it. Mortgage away.

- Once you own your first home, get a raise and make sure your spouse gets a raise too, because you need to decorate.

- Once you have your dream home of the moment squared away, obsess about getting pregnant.

- Once you are pregnant, set up your gift registry for your baby shower, and then meticulously put together a Pinterest-perfect pink or blue nursery and prepare a wardrobe filled with pink or blue onesies.

- Once you have children, repeat the process of making more money, finding a new dream home, and decorating.

Then what?

After you conquer the Disney Princess wish list, it can feel like there are no more major occasions to look forward to. This can make getting older seem a bit depressing. I got to a point where I didn't even want to celebrate my birthday, because every year just meant more crow's feet and less fun.

Luckily, with a little perspective, I realized the silliness of the whole thing and snapped out of the aging-phobia phase pretty quickly. I now embrace getting older and love celebrating every passing year. The French way of life is not about achieving goals and celebrating big milestones but about enjoying the little things and celebrating whenever you feel like it. The French emphasize living in the actual moment instead of living for certain major life moments. Yes, getting older is a big deal if you really dwell upon it, but the French have a glorious way of turning important things into trivial things and vice versa. They sweat the small stuff. The rest? Shrug. Facts are not very important, but the process of forming conclusions about these facts sure is, and that is a beautiful thing because you can rationalize away the things that are bothering you and just enjoy the rest. You can live completely in the abstract if you feel like it.

So the answer to "Then what?" is "Have fun."

A Parisienne who partied a lot in her twenties doesn't wake up one day in the suburbs in a big house with a bigger mortgage, surrounded by a husband and children and things, but completely lacking interesting experiences and fun nights out with friends. Her life can go on almost as it did before children. Why would she not continue to go to parties after having kids?

Once coupled, Americans tend to move away from their single stomping grounds in the name of more space and better schools for the kids. Credit-card bills and car payments often take priority over having a roster of regular babysitters and taking vacations. Dinner is served earlier and earlier, and the TV stays on longer.

No matter a French woman's financial situation, she figures out a way to have some independence and adequate childcare. She probably doesn't own a home with walk-in closets, but she keeps her friends and her career. She is present for her children, but her children do not define her.

My friend Christine, an American who has lived in Paris for nearly a decade, has a great job, a wonderful husband, and two adorable young children. Far away from her upbringing in the United States, she has learned that, yes, there are sacrifices to be made when becoming a mother—lack of sleep and lack of space—but she does not need to forgo fun dinners out with friends and much-needed family vacations.

Once at a dinner party at Christine's apartment, I chatted with an interesting French couple. They described some recent late-night revelry, and because they had three children, I assumed it was one of those one-off stories that we tend to tell at parties. After we finished dinner at midnight, my husband and I were shocked that they were all going out afterward. They were shocked that we weren't. We had to get home to the babysitter, and the thought of having a hangover and dealing with a tempestuous two-year-old the next morning terrified us. Not only did it not even occur to me to say yes, but I totally judged them. What kind of parents stay out super late at night, dancing on banquettes?

This kind, apparently. Paris and New York have had their way with me, and I couldn't be more thankful. In the words of Benjamin Franklin, "there will be sleeping enough in the grave."

When my daughter was in the baby and toddler stages, I went for long stretches of time without the opportunity to let loose on the dance floor (which I adore) because that was just not the married life that I had set up for myself. It was also not what I thought responsible mothers did, probably because my mother rarely went out and had fun while raising me. Luckily she too has seen the light, and she now goes dancing with her boyfriend at least two nights per week. It's never too late to change old routines and spice up your life.

Nightlife actually originated in Paris due to people literally being able to see the light, thanks to Louis XIV. Paris was the first city anywhere to regularly, and permanently, light up its streets at night. Prior to this, no cities in the world glittered after dark, and the dead of the night was considered to be 9:00 p.m.

Far from being just a beautification project, Paris's becoming the City of Light had an extreme impact, forever changing the rhythm of society. Can you imagine wandering around any large city at night in complete darkness? *Ce n'est pas bon.* Lights make city streets safe and therefore good for commerce and entertainment. Before the end of Louis XIV's reign, Parisians started feeling comfortable and enjoying life on the newly lit streets at all hours, long before residents of other cities such as London did.[5] So Paris became the original city that never sleeps centuries before New York could take claim.

I have never had more fun than I have in the past few years, and I owe it all to French women and my fellow faux Frenchies. If you decide to have children, or already have, figure out a way to have sexy nights out with your significant other and laughter-filled nights out with friends. These don't need to be wild and crazy; they can just include going out to eat more, joining clubs or groups that align with your interests, or making an effort to invite a group of friends over for dinner once a month.

Prior to Paris's realization of its full potential as the City of Light, dinner parties as we know them didn't exist. They couldn't.

Friends had to leave each other's homes early or otherwise face heading home in a very threatening environment. But after the revolutionary night-lighting concept went into place, going to visit friends and escorting friends home became an extension of the evening's entertainment. For example, the famed Marquise de Sévigné threw an animated dinner party that lasted until after midnight in December of 1673 at her apartment just off the Place des Vosges.[6] Nightlife had arrived.

Life's short, so enjoy your town's well-lit streets, and have fun!

Relative to the conventional American way, the European way is to own less and do more. Thankfully the American version is slowly changing as the sharing economy is replacing our credit culture. Globally, cities are overtaking the suburbs, paving the way for services like Lyft and Airbnb to encourage renting over buying (and renting only what will be used). While 40 percent of the world's population lived in cities in 1980, the number is expected to be more than 60 percent by 2030. That adds up to more than sixty million urbanites each year. By 2050, seven out of ten people in the world will live in a city.[7] In comparison to suburban life, there's something about city culture that places a high value on travel and enjoyable meals at restaurants with friends.

La joie de vivre is all about savoring these moments. You can practice this by paying more attention to the quality of meals and their surroundings, taking the time to talk and enjoy an *apéritif* before dinner, and lingering longer over weekend lunches.

Naturally, the concept of setting aside a time and place just for culinary pleasures can be traced back to the Louies, as can so many components of what we still consider refinement to be. The first restaurant scene developed in Paris during Louis XIV's reign. Before the advent of French *haute cuisine*, homes did not contain dining rooms. Vaux-le-Vicomte was the first château with a dining room, which was very avant-garde in 1661. Louis XIV ate most of his meals alone in his bedroom, as Versailles didn't have a room reserved for dining at the time. Its halls were more appropriate for entertaining on a large scale. In 1735, Louis XV set aside a space at Versailles reserved exclusively for dining, and it was only during this century that dining rooms began to become common.[8]

Another remnant lesson from the Versailles era is to fully and wholeheartedly celebrate beauty. However, the modern-day version of that sentiment is to cherish the beauty of everything, whether perfect or imperfect, gilded or weathered.

Growing up in California, I lived in homes that all had smooth white walls and ceilings: clean but clinical. We refreshed the rooms every few years and remodeled every decade. In Paris, walls and ceilings throughout the city are alive. You can see beautiful cherubs and other intricate designs but also cracked paint and water leaks. The walls and ceilings may not be spotless, but they're interesting. Every room tells a story, and if you want to learn it, all you have to do is look up. Old buildings have long histories, just like vintage clothing and antique furniture does. In Paris, things are rarely replaced, so you see layers of personality and *joie de vivre*, every layer adding to the greater narrative of the city itself.

Chapter 5

Ungilding the Lily

You'd be hard-pressed to find something more emulated and reproduced than the elements of French interior design. Prior to Versailles, French interiors did not hold court as worldwide dominator, but Louis XIV ensured that the display at his home became the most coveted. Versailles of course created an impact because of its over-the-top ornateness, but more importantly, because it was open to the public from the beginning instead of being hidden in private; it played host to many a wide-eyed visitor.

Humorously, Versailles has been replicated by an overzealous businessman in China and by a train wreck of a couple in Florida, the latter project awesomely chronicled in the documentary *The Queen of Versailles*. While these attempts to buy taste induce cringing, imitation is the sincerest form of flattery, and in the case of something as gorgeous as Versailles, it's actually understandable. It's human nature to desire an upgrade in status, but in the past, that would have remained a dream or become the reality of just a few. Today, upgrades in socioeconomic status in the United States and in emerging markets have become relatively commonplace, and so it is only natural to try to buy the fast-track pass to elegance.

Because of rapid wealth creation and accumulation, the digital revolution, and the relative ease and affordability of travel, the process of developing a level of taste that is deemed acceptable by high society has sped up dramatically. And the obvious starting places are Versailles and Paris—but the opulent Instagram versions, not the real ones.

Whether it's the curved lines of Louis XV or the straight ones of Louis XVI, traditional French style is bar none the ultimate in the world of furniture and interior decorating. Louis XIV tossed aside previous notions of furnishings, particularly in that his goal was to show off his wealth and power instead of religious reverence. The furniture was elaborately constructed just outside of Paris using impressive materials such as brass, ivory, and exotic Japanese lacquer. New design motifs from the Sun King's era include the famous fleur-de-lis and the very look-at-me-I'm-Louis interlocking Ls and sunbursts. Slight curves and heavy Italian baroque influences also mark the Louis XIV style.

Furniture under the reign of Louis XV became more elaborate. Designers exaggerated curves, emphasized comfort, and somewhat abandoned symmetry. Key motifs were flowers, shells, and chinoiserie. Under Louis XVI, symmetry and classicism returned with a vengeance. Whereas a curved marble fireplace with a shell design in the center can immediately be recognized as Louis XV, more restrained pieces whose structural lines are all straight can be pinned as Louis XVI.

With interior design, as well as with fashion and food and really anything in which styles evolve, the upper echelons of society adopt a particular trend specifically to differentiate themselves from the lower levels. Then the masses eventually discover and copy the style in an attempt to appear to be part of a higher class, and at this point, the upper classes move on to the next iteration. German sociologist Georg Simmel called this progression the trickle-down process. But by the end of Louis XVI's reign, the social hierarchy was toppled on its head, and many of the upper classes literally lost their heads. So the notion of an upper class became a bit fuzzy for some time, and this, I theorize, is one of the reasons that the taste of Versailles and the Louies has been frozen in time and emblazoned into our global consciousness. When over-the-top glamour and court life returned to fashion under Emperor Napoléon III, no new style appeared. His wife, Eugénie, had quite an obsession with Marie Antoinette, so the royal residences were decorated in Louis XVI style.

Fast-forward to modern-day Paris, and the style is, well, modern. Clean-lined modern furniture and contemporary art work extraordinarily well in spaces that have such life and character to begin with. In many nice Parisian apartments, ornate marble fireplaces topped with original speckled, mercury-filled mirrors are *de rigueur,* and intricate decorative flourishes from the early 1900s often remain intact, so simple furnishings really pop against this stunning backdrop. If you see an entire apartment decorated in the style of Louis Quatorze, you know that it belongs to either someone over the age of sixty or, more likely, a foreigner.

Contemporary furniture, art, and decorative pieces are common, as are midcentury modern pieces (French, Italian, and American). Art deco—architecture and decorative arts created between the First and Second World Wars—is also a very popular style seen in chic apartments, hotels, and restaurants throughout Paris. Just as with clothing, it's not cool to do a total look or be too matchy-matchy. It is very common in

Parisian apartments to spice up the modern and contemporary décor with items purchased from travels around the globe. Think African rugs and trinkets from Thailand.

Interiors aside, a big part of what makes Paris so appealing today is the uniformity and permanence of its exterior architecture. At the risk of sounding like a cheesy design blog that deems everything French *ah-mazing*, I consider Parisian architecture to be the epitome of timelessness and elegance. I'm going to say it anyway, because seriously, it is.

But it wasn't always this way. Paris used to be, by many accounts, positively medieval until major developments in the seventeenth and nineteenth centuries changed pretty much everything. There was an interlude in the rebuilding of Paris in the eighteenth century during the reign of Louis XV.

In the seventeenth century, wood was declared unsafe for home building because it created fire hazards, but it remained prevalent because it was relatively inexpensive. Building with wood began to change, however, with the lavish residences designed by Louis Le Vau on the Île Saint-Louis. Whereas stone had previously been reserved for royal palaces, the wealthy new residents of the fashionable island started building homes entirely of light stone, which looked incredibly sophisticated at the time and still does today. The most costly homes used *pierre de taille* stone—cut and finished with square edges and smooth faces—and now this look appears throughout Paris. It has become a big part of what defines the classic Parisian look.[9]

In the nineteenth century, Napoléon III (who was called Louis-Napoléon before he made himself emperor) was determined to create a lasting legacy. He wanted to be to Paris what Augustus was to Rome. He, along with the man he appointed to carry out most of the work, Baron Georges-Eugène Haussmann (who made himself a baron), certainly succeeded in making a permanent mark on Paris. Called the *grands travaux*, the massive urban renovation project undertaken by these two men turned Paris into a seemingly never-ending construction site.

Between 1852 and 1870, more than 20 percent of the city's population was forced to move because of the work, and twenty-seven thousand buildings were knocked down. During this same period, more than one hundred thousand houses were built, and many of them were high-end apartment buildings. On each block, the buildings were supposed to have the same main façade lines, the same heights between floors, and the same style of roof, covered in slate. These rules resulted in what is still known as a "Haussmannian apartment building," a seven-story stone building with a regular pattern of windows and a frontage of at least fifty feet, built in stone with wrought-iron *balcons*, cornices, and moldings. Either the second or the third story is taller than the others, creating what is called the *étage noble*. The buildings contain courtyards for ventilation, and the interiors are fairly consistent in layout and design.[10]

As is the case with any type of progress in Paris, reviews of Haussmann's radical and relatively speedy renovations were mixed at the time. Although many historical buildings—even entire city blocks—were razed in the name of improved circulation and uniformity, Paris would simply not be Paris without this period of brazen urban planning. And although Paris's current architectural state is certainly not only attributable to Napoléon III and Haussmann, it probably wouldn't have been possible if not for their determination and single-minded convictions. Believe it or not, Haussmann was not even an aesthete, but he was certainly efficient and effective.

When I first visited Paris, the thing that struck me the most was the overwhelming beauty of the architecture. And not just the architecture in one area but everywhere I looked. That's still true every time I set foot in the city. Yes, there are plenty of charming hidden corners and grand gilded monuments, but really what makes central Paris's appearance so stunning is its consistency. Because of the sheer number of buildings that were constructed under Haussmann's watchful eye, with the style and composition more or less replicated from one building to the next, Paris has a sense of architectural harmony that is hard for other large cities to top.

But the progress made in the seventeenth century should not be overlooked. If you want to see Parisian architecture that predates Haussmann, head to the Marais, where you can still admire delightfully crooked mansions featuring charming wooden beams.

Another appealing aspect of Paris is its order and cleanliness. Whereas in New York and California it can be hard to see where your tax dollars go, in central Paris, it's right in front of your face. The Parisian government constantly sweeps its streets, immediately fixes its potholes, and keeps its parks in pristine condition.

If you have a chance, I suggest you kick things off on the Île Saint-Louis by eating a little Berthillon ice cream and watching some *pierre de taille*. Then stroll through the Marais to the Place des Vosges, one of the seventeenth century's triumphs. Centuries later, there are still few better ways to spend an afternoon than parking yourself on a bench under its meticulously groomed trees.

Chapter 6

Bon Voyage

Long before the age of Haussmann and Napoléon III, the upper classes took vacations that involved travel, but that practice died out with the fall of the Roman Empire. Notable trips in the Middle Ages and Renaissance era were few and far between, and when people did travel, they did so for a specific purpose and never just to see the sights. People did not travel again for pleasure until Louis XIV reworked Paris into a city that just had to be seen.[11]

Today, Paris is still one of the most visited cities in the world. One of the main attractions—and perhaps the city's most iconic symbol—is the Eiffel Tower. When you think of Paris, what is the first image that pops into your head? For me, it's *la Tour Eiffel.* The sparkling version, of course.

It all began with the approaching arrival of the World's Fair in 1889, in which Paris was preparing to celebrate the one-hundred-year anniversary of the French Revolution. Eiffel et Compagnie, a construction firm owned by renowned architect and metals expert Alexandre-Gustave Eiffel, was commissioned to construct a grand monument that would serve as the entrance to the exposition. It took several hundred workers and two years to complete the tower by March of 1889. At the time, it was the tallest structure in the world, making it a topic of much discussion and debate. Many Parisians considered the new monument to be an eyesore. The writer Guy de Maupassant apparently hated the tower so much that he often ate lunch in the restaurant at its base, the only vantage point from which he could completely avoid glimpsing its looming silhouette.[12] Never short on strong opinions, those Parisians.

La Tour Eiffel was originally intended to be temporary, and it was almost torn down in 1909, but city officials decided to save it, only after recognizing its value as a radiotelegraph station. It was almost torn down again when Hitler ordered its demolition,[13] but luckily that command was never carried out. Now nearly seven million people per year visit this tower of intricately latticed iron, making it the world's most visited monument that people pay to enter. Can you imagine Paris today without it? For me, seeing it offers instant gratification.

Viewing the Eiffel Tower up close in the Champ de Mars (a large public green space in the seventh arrondissement) is the best way to understand its size and power. It appears far from delicate from this vantage point because you can feel the full effect of all of that hearty ironwork. Little details that you never noticed before pop out. Suddenly you realize that you never thought of its color before, but now it becomes clear that *la Tour Eiffel* is not just bare iron; it is coated in bronze paint.

In fact, the monument has been repainted eighteen times since its construction and has changed colors several times, from reddish brown to yellow ochre to chestnut brown to the bronze of today. It is shaded differently at the top to ensure that viewers perceive the color to be the same throughout as it stands against the Paris sky.[14]

During the nightly on-the-hour five minutes of sparkle, the natural inclination is to stare at the Eiffel Tower and watch the show or to kiss a loved one. Or kiss someone you just met because this is Paris, after all. But if you exit the Champ de Mars and walk around the seventh arrondissement during this time, you're in for a treat. The reflection of the tower's sparkling lights dances off every single window on the surrounding apartment buildings, which makes your eyes widen with wonder. You hold your breath for an extra second, you notice your heartbeat, and you enjoy the moment of pure delight. Wow. Just wow.

Across the Seine, over in the sixteenth arrondissement, you can find a completely different perspective at the Place du Trocadéro. This is where you see all of those photos of people pretending to hold the Eiffel Tower in their hands or standing next to it while giving it a big kiss. I'm not really into touristy stuff, but this is special because it offers the ideal photo op. If you bring back one thing from Paris, make it a picture with *la Tour Eiffel* behind you because you will cherish it forever.

Though it would be difficult to find a Parisian who gets excited about seeing the Eiffel Tower (except perhaps if it is the view from an acquaintance's apartment, in which case this is more resentment than excitement), all Parisians get fired up about traveling and talking about traveling. Throw in a complaint about the weather and perhaps some juicy gossip along with your travel talk, and you've just mastered the art of local banter.

But, of course, in order to talk about travel, it helps to actually travel, and that they do. Not only do they have the time off from work, but also destinations within Europe and North Africa are just a few hours and a cheap flight away. The art of travel became culturally ingrained in France after the implementation of the 1936 Matignon

Agreements, a.k.a. *Les Accords de Matignon*, a.k.a. the Magna Carta of French Labor. Among other things, these laws granted workers two weeks of paid vacation for the first time in France.

Now the average full-time employed European receives about five weeks' paid leave per year, while workers in the United States are not guaranteed the legal right to any vacation time at all. Many American companies provide longer-term workers with two weeks off per year, but 40 percent of Americans do not use up their entire allotment, according to the US Travel Association.[15] The Center for Economic Policy and Research declared that the United States is the only rich nation without legally mandated vacations for employees.[16]

I once had a job in Southern California that allowed me five days of sick and vacation leave combined for the entire year. (I was vice president of marketing communications for a company that promoted—wait for it—travel.) Clearly, that job was not very conducive to global exploration. French people would revolt in the same situation. Meanwhile, approximately one-third of Americans don't have passports.

Dreaming about and talking about travel is a quintessential part of being Parisian. Destinations with top bragging rights include New York (especially Brooklyn), Thailand, and anywhere in Latin America. In Paris, your *copains* and coworkers seriously envy you if you can regale them with recent experiences in Brooklyn, Bangkok, and Buenos Aires all in one conversation.

Completely different—more comfortable than cool—is the strong cultural link between France and Morocco, which I picked up on early in my journey as a Francophile. Just like Californians love their tacos and burritos, the French love a good tagine.

Moroccan and French interaction dates back to the eighth century, when battles about land and religion took place in Southern France. Cultural exchanges followed. Fast-forward a few centuries, and Morocco gained its independence from France in a relatively amicable way. Both cultural and economic ties between the two countries are close but complex. France is Morocco's primary trade partner, but relations aren't always friendly. There have been wars, and then there was Javier Bardem. Clearly it did not go over well when it was widely reported that French diplomat Gérard Araud allegedly told the actor that "Morocco is a mistress who you sleep with every night, who you don't particularly love but you have to defend" in 2014.[17]

Today, Morocco is a sovereign state governed by King Mohammed VI. Located in North Africa, it is a part of what is called the Maghreb region. A trip there requires a little sense of adventure but not much. Foreign yet westernized, exotic yet safe, Morocco is instantly enticing, with its architecturally fascinating domes, lush courtyards, intricately cut dark wood panels, and brightly colored tiles. You will find the five-times-a-day prayer calls blaring out from the nearest minaret to be jarring at first but then comforting by day two, pleasant and poetic reminders that you're far away from home. Your eyes will wander over the bold but delicate Arabic calligraphy scrolled across every sign.

The distinct smell of double apple will waft by, and you'll turn to see men in long djellaba robes puffing on shisha pipes, decorating the air with tufts of thick white smoke. As you walk into the souk, the double-apple smell will transform into a strong, sensual, woodsy one—oud—which will then be replaced by a veritable orgy of the senses once you enter the spices section. There will be mounds and mounds of spices, everywhere you look. You will feel alive and tranquil all at once, thanks to the rhythmic instrumental music playing in the background, its melody enchanting and trancelike. And that's all before you spot the snake charmers.

Because Moroccan food is both exotic and delicious, I fell in love with it at first bite. There really isn't anything that compares with the fragrant smells and peppery spices of slow-cooked North

African meats and tagines, which are particularly great for fall and winter. At home, if you pull up a Moroccan lounge playlist on Spotify and labor over an aromatic tagine, I guarantee that you will feel transported to a faraway place, not in reality, but in the depths of your imagination. One whiff of ras el hanout spices, argan oil, mint tea, orange blossom water, or rose water, and I'm right back in Marrakech. If you have problems finding anything in your local market for your culinary experimentation, Amazon is a virtual treasure trove of foreign food delights, Moroccan or otherwise.

Years ago, I received a Le Creuset cast-iron tagine base and earthenware coned lid as a gift, and I started trying out recipes that came with the enclosed cookbook. I began with salty, sweet lemon chicken and then moved on to vegetable tagines starring harissa and beef ones dotted with green olives. But one day my husband decided to make one, which turned out to be astronomically better than any of mine, so he is now the official tagine maker in our household. Below is his recipe for lamb tagine, which has become one of our favorite warm meals for cold days.

Lamb Tagine with Fennel and Dates
Prep time: 30 minutes, plus overnight marinating
Cook time: 4 hours (best made in advance)
Serves 8

4 pounds leg of lamb (with bone)
2 cups chicken broth (Pacific organic free-range chicken broth is our favorite, but any kind will work)
10 Medjool dates, cut in half, pits removed
3 large fennel bulbs, cut into large pieces
2 large white onions, sliced
8 medium carrots, ends and tips trimmed
cilantro leaves, stems removed

extra-virgin olive oil
3 tablespoons garlic, chopped
freshly ground black pepper
fine sea salt

Mix the following dry ingredients together for the marinade:
4 teaspoons ground ginger
8 teaspoons ground cumin
8 teaspoons ground coriander
2 teaspoons Espelette pepper
2 teaspoons chili powder
2 teaspoons cayenne pepper
2 teaspoons paprika
1 teaspoon cinnamon
2 teaspoons fine sea salt

Mix the dry spices listed above in a medium-sized glass bowl, and then add 8 tablespoons of olive oil and 3 tablespoons of chopped garlic. Place the leg of lamb into a large 1-gallon Ziploc bag and pour the entire marinade on top. Remove any excess air from the bag and seal it. Place a second 1-gallon Ziploc bag over the first bag, remove any air, and seal. Once both bags are sealed, massage the mixture into the meat to ensure that the marinade covers the entire leg of lamb. Place in the refrigerator overnight (or a minimum of 3 hours).

Wash and prep the vegetables, and preheat the oven to 325 degrees (Fahrenheit).

Coat the bottom of a Dutch oven with olive oil. (You will use this same pot for the entire cooking process; no need to clean in between steps). Place the Dutch oven on the stovetop on high heat. Add the sliced onions and stir until they brown to a dark caramel color. Turn the heat down to medium and add the fennel. Season the onions and fennel with a few pinches of salt and pepper (and add more olive oil if needed); stir and cook until fennel is soft. Remove onions and fennel, place into a large glass bowl, and set aside.

Add a bit more oil to the now-empty Dutch oven and place on high heat. Once hot, add the marinated lamb to brown for 30 seconds on each side. Remove the lamb and place on top of the onions and fennel. Turn off the burner and line the bottom of the empty Dutch oven with the carrots. Cover with the chicken broth just to the top of the carrots. Place browned lamb on top and season with a few generous pinches of salt and pepper. Cover the sides and top of the lamb with fennel and onions, and put the lid on the Dutch oven.

Note: It is normal for the tagine to drip a bit, so as a precaution, place an aluminum-lined baking sheet under the pot before placing it in the oven to catch any drips.

Place the pot (with lid) onto an aluminum-lined baking sheet and bake at 325 degrees for 2 hours. After 2 hours, carefully remove from the oven, along with the baking sheet, and add more chicken broth as needed to ensure the pot does not burn. Be careful not to overfill the pot. Place back into the oven and bake for another hour. After 1 hour (3 hours total), remove again from the oven and drain any excessive fat off the top of the pot. Rotate the lamb, but be careful not to move the carrots on the bottom; just move the lamb. Season the lamb with a few pinches of salt and pepper.

Add the dates and mix slightly with the fennel and onions. Add more chicken broth if needed, cover, and place back into the oven. Cook for another hour, and then remove from the heat after 4 hours. Drain extra fat off the top with a spoon or baster. Remove the bone from the lamb and let the meat sit for 30 minutes in the pot. Strain any remaining fat and place everything else into a deep serving dish with a lid.

It is best to separate the finished dish into three sections (carrots, lamb, and fennel/onions) to allow for easy serving. Top with fresh cilantro and serve with couscous.

Feel free to make it one day ahead because the flavors really come together. Moroccan food is all about hospitality, conviviality, and abundance, so invite some friends over and share the love.

Chapter 7

City of Love

The divide between the English and the French goes back centuries. Bitter wars were fought, and relations still haven't recovered. The rudeness of the "French frogs" is indoctrinated into the English mind-set, and the French are certainly not doing anything to change their snobbish reputation. Among countless other disparities, French people dress sleekly and simply, while in England it's more fashionable to look a bit eccentric or quirky. French manners are distant and clipped, while Brits are effusively apologetic and polite. Prolific photographer and noted world traveler Henri Cartier-Bresson once said that England is the most exotic country for a Frenchman because it is so different.

My ancestors are from the United Kingdom, and in Paris I'm often asked if I'm English. Once I assure them, "*Non, je suis américaine,*" the snarl goes away and the taxi driver's or sales associate's face instantly softens a bit, and then he or she inevitably launches into a description of a favorite American TV show or a cousin who just visited New York. While French people have varying opinions about *les américains*—all strong ones—at least we are the ones they hate to love, versus the English, whom they love to hate.

One of the most noticeable elements of the divide across the Channel is that of romance. While French people's prowess in the *amour* department needs no introduction, the English are often outwardly reserved when it comes to sex, love, and the expression of emotions. When uncomfortable, they make a joke. My family passed down this English approach for generations. Whenever any couple held hands or kissed in public, my father made a point to declare that they should "get a room." The message was drilled in over and over: jokes are fine, but real romance—if there is any—should be a private matter.

No wonder French culture is so appealing. In Paris, there are innuendos around every corner, fueling feelings of liberation and hedonism. French people don't need to be tipsy in order to flirt. Sexual tension and lingering stares between strangers swirl around the city like magical pixie dust—at parties, in restaurants, on the *métro*. Then there's the whole Marquis de Sade thing. And steamy affairs are just par for the course; wedding rings are seen as yellow lights, not red ones.

In eighteenth-century Paris, pre-Revolutionary intellectuals known as *libertins* denounced religious conventions like chastity and monogamy, as Heather Stimmler-Hall points out in her book *Naughty Paris: A Lady's Guide to the Sexy City*. "As opposition to the Church and King continued to grow, support for legalized prostitution and liberal sexual practices spread through the city's fashionable circles." After the Revolution, the new empire regulated brothels, which were filled with registered employees who received weekly health inspections. More than 180 of these *maisons de tolerance* were operating in Paris by 1810.[18]

Outside of brothels, café terraces were the ultimate strategic places for soliciting prostitutes, who could be seen from inside and from the streets. At "absinthe time" in the early evening, they sat at tables with a drink and waited for customers, cigarette in hand, as depicted by Degas, Manet, and Van Gogh. Cabarets, especially the famous Moulin Rouge and Folies-Bergère, were also epicenters for prostitution. Further up the sexual social ladder was the Paris Opéra, which was frequented by the upper-middle classes and the aristocracy. The opera became a prime venue for high-class prostitution, particularly during carnival time before Lent, when racy masked balls were held every Saturday evening. The *demimondaines*—those at the top of said ladder—were admired at the opera and noted by the press. They often started out in the theater to show off their beauty, even if they had no real talent. For their high-society patrons, keeping a *demimondaine* was a sign of virility and wealth.[19]

The more money these women had lavished on them, the more they spent and the more their expenses grew. Saving was not part of the deal because mistresses were meant to be flaunted, not hidden. As a result, they more or less intermingled with high society, and they weren't easily identified by their appearances. Society observers at the time claimed that it was difficult to tell if the *demimondaines* were dressing like honest women or if honest women were dressing like the *demimondaines*. Meanwhile, over in New York, a completely different attitude prevailed, where the goal was to stamp out prostitution completely.[20]

All of this provocative history has turned Paris into the ideal backdrop for romance and desire. People who visit the city can easily fall in lust or in love, whether for the first time or all over again. How can you not feel sexy in a city where everyone looks like he or she has just had sex?

As Caroline de Maigret, Audrey Diwan, Sophie Mas, and Anne Berest emphasize in their book, *How to Be Parisian Wherever You Are: Love, Style, and Bad Habits,*

Always be fuckable: when standing in line at the bakery on a Sunday morning, buying champagne in the middle of the night, or even picking the kids up from school. You never know.[21]

Angéline Mélin

Chapter 8

....

The Paris Syndrome

When you are searching for an apartment in Paris, it can come as a surprise that the current owners or tenants are often present (and often cranky) during the viewings, which is awkward to say the least. People trying to sell or rent their homes do not throw open houses, and not everyone tidies up before private showings. The process offers a quick primer—or more like a baptism by fire—on how Parisians really live.

During my apartment search in Paris before I made the leap from Newport Beach, I noticed that many of the master bathrooms had bras and panties hanging to dry. Once I got over the initial astonishment that women didn't hide their underthings when they knew strangers would be traipsing through their apartments, I realized that I could simply wash my lingerie in the shower with me each morning. I had been sticking them in a mesh bag in the washing machine and then hanging them up to dry, but I had watched delicate trims, such as lace, slowly disintegrate with each wash.

Now I wash the previous day's worn item in the shower, hang it on a towel to dry, buy nice lingerie items, and keep them in pristine condition year after year. Save your mesh bags for your clothing instead of using them for lingerie. I also immensely cut down on dry cleaning after discovering The Laundress Crease Release and Fabric Fresh. While there once was a time when I would send out my "dry clean only" clothing after one or two wears, now I simply spray Fabric Fresh on the garment and hang it back up in my closet smelling as good as new. If an item becomes wrinkled, especially from being rolled up in a suitcase, I spray Crease Release all over it, shake it out, *et voilà,* no wrinkles!

You're probably thinking, "What does this have to do with Paris?" Though these laundering tips seem trivial, the approach sums up a major difference between Americans and the French. We toss what they keep. A Parisienne doesn't rack up big dry cleaning, shopping, or grooming bills in the way that her New York counterpart does. The especially American pattern of constant consumption has stayed ever present since the postwar era and has rapidly expanded to other countries as well. We are incessantly inundated with messages about new things to buy.

Throwaway consumerism is rampant in the United States but not in France. Whether it's food or fashion, French people generally buy carefully and use what they buy. They value experiences over material items. Things don't need to be luxurious, just adequate, allowing them to spend more on meals or trips with friends.

By contrast, opulence is a big component of the French fantasy for foreigners. Books, shows, and movies often portray Paris as an over-the-top luxe playground. But that part is really just for tourists. You don't see this when you visit Paris on vacation; it took me months to realize what a "real" Parisian's life is like. He doesn't live like Jean-Paul. After my single-girl-does-Paris trip, which fueled these stereotypes in my mind even further (and now probably yours...sorry!), the slow realization that this was an exception and not the norm came as quite a surprise.

I think many Americans envision French people sitting around nibbling on caviar and foie gras, but the French earn an average of approximately 2,200 euros per month (under $30,000 per year).[22] Youth unemployment remains high at 24.4 percent,[23] and under-employment is a problem.

I've seen every kind of Parisian way of living, from the bottom to the top, and even at the top, people still have an innate sense of value. It is not a wasteful culture, and in it luxury is something to be hidden and a bit embarrassed by. (Though it should be noted here that—as with New York City and Southern California—there is a vast difference between Paris and the French Riviera in this aspect; the latter is all about glitz and glamour.) A real Parisienne's life does not look like what you've read in guidebooks and seen in movies.

angeline Mélin

The modern French mind-set was established during the Revolution. Parisians are frugal and practical. Meanwhile, the rest of the world clings to the gilded Versailles vision of France, all Champagne towers and layers upon layers of macaron-colored garments.

Though the Revolution seems like ancient history, it was a recent occurrence in France, relatively speaking. The United States is a toddler compared to France, and the events surrounding the birth of the United States are still very relevant to the modern American mind-set. Both countries are theoretically founded upon many of the same principles, but Americans emphasize the *liberté* while the French emphasize the *fraternité*. Strikes in the street in Paris are still commonplace, and we know that—we see them in the news; we make jokes about them—but why are they celebrated? To understand the reasoning is to understand the French. Asserting revolutionary heritage is of the utmost importance.

Putting the nuisances of strikes aside, French solidarity is a really beautiful thing to witness. A strong sense of place pervades all aspects of life in this prideful country. Powerful feelings about *les droits de l'homme* (human rights) hang like watchful clouds over every conversation and every decision. Fairness trumps all. In a time of crisis, there is nowhere better to be than surrounded by French people, who instantly kick into *fraternité* mode and will go to any length to help out a fellow human being.

Marie Antoinette may be a symbol of France, but she was beheaded and does not at all represent the mentality of French people today. They're still metaphorically storming the Bastille while we're wandering around the Hall of Mirrors, taking selfies. Sure, we've studied the Revolution, but what do we want to remember, Robespierre or royalty? The Sofia Coppola version of the story is breathtaking, but the film doesn't show the people's struggle leading up to, or after, the fall of the monarchy and subsequent rejection of its luxurious trappings. During the time of the Louies, yes, Paris had some spectacular buildings, but much of the rest of it was filled with scenes of poverty, its cramped streets narrow and filthy. The pre-Revolutionary Versailles version is certainly a much more palatable visual for visitors than that of Parisians parading around with aristocrats' heads on pikes. The guillotine may be long gone, but resentment toward the wealthy still exists.

A real Parisienne is more Rosie the Riveter than Marie Antoinette. Parisians take comfort in being resilient and a bit pessimistic. A surly waiter is not necessarily considered to be a bad one.

This discrepancy between tourists' lavish assumptions and the more sober reality is the cause of an actual thing called "Paris Syndrome," in which some Japanese tourists experience psychiatric breakdowns upon arrival in Paris because the city does not meet their expectations. The Japanese embassy even set up a twenty-four-hour hotline for those suffering from severe culture shock. Japanese psychiatrist Hiroaki Ota first identified the syndrome decades ago.[24]

Symptoms can include dizziness, delusions, and hallucinations sometimes so serious that the traveler must be flown back home under medical supervision. While this extreme reaction probably seems preposterous to Westerners, the underlying cause is something that can rattle any first-time traveler. As Chelsea Fagan points out in the *Atlantic*, watching movies about Paris leads viewers to believe that the city is affluent, quaint, and friendly:

We imagine the whole city just smells like Chanel No. 5 and has a government-mandated mime on every corner. And nowhere is this narrow view of Paris more prevalent than in Japan, where the media portrays the city as one filled with thin, gorgeous, unbelievably rich citizens. The three stops of a Parisian's day, according to the Japanese media, are a café, the Eiffel Tower, and Louis Vuitton. Yet, despite our international desire to imagine that this is a city where pigeons stay in the parks and the waiters occasionally burst into song, Paris can be a harsh place...And while this does not stop Paris from being a wonderful, beautiful city—every city has its pros and cons—the fact that its downsides are wiped so institutionally clean from the media isn't doing it any favors. Unlike New York, which embraces its gritty underbelly in its public image—"Hey, you might get shot walking to the post office, but that's what makes it fun!"—the world seems determined to represent Paris as perpetually spinning inside a little girl's music box.[25]

During my time living in Paris—which I found to be harsh on some days and postcard-perfect on others—I learned to better appreciate all of the little things that make life good. And that, really, is the best thing about spending time in France.

Denial and delays are such a big part of Parisian life that you are forced to slow down and surrender. If you try to rationalize why something should be open, why something should work, or why something should be easier or faster, you will go crazy. So you stop. And maybe you take a break from being pissed off that your Wi-Fi is out yet again, and you focus instead on the delicious yogurt that you're eating for breakfast. You know that this yogurt does not exist anywhere else outside France, and yet here, you can buy some at every Monoprix. It's not sweet like American yogurt or tangy like Greek yogurt; it's just right. So you shrug about the Wi-Fi and savor every bite, drizzling on one last drop of honey from Provence.

Chapter 9

....

Watching the World Go By

Understanding the art of *flânerie* is a crucial part of understanding Paris. The poet Charles Baudelaire defined the term *flâneur* as a passionate wanderer-spectator whose habitat is the crowd.[26] The female version is a *flâneuse.* Next time you find yourself in a crowded place, surrender to the moment and give it a try.

Because I lived in Paris, I've become some sort of de facto guide for anyone I've ever met in my life who happens to be going there, whether friend or acquaintance or acquaintance of acquaintance. Typically, he or she e-mails me some sort of packed itinerary that is full of this and full of that. It's about going efficiently from Point A to Point B and then on to the next European city's Point A to Point B, Griswold-style. But where is the time for wandering about and doing nothing? Should I slot it in for them?

In Paris, you can do nothing and see everything. There doesn't need to be a Point B. Satisfaction is the destination.

Whenever anyone asks me, "What should I do in Paris?" or "What is the best place to eat in Paris?" or "What should I see in Paris?" my

answer is generally the same. Though I do try to provide a few tailored, specific places of interest if requested, as long as you steer clear of the tourist traps, everything and anything is the best thing to do or eat or see in Paris. Every major metropolitan city is fascinating to walk through and discover, but in my mind, nowhere beats Paris. I did it every day for two years, and I still can't wait to go back for more, which is something that I do often. It never gets old.

In New York, things open and have their moment, and then they fade and go out of business; in Paris, things get old, and they become respected, albeit respected places that are frequented by tourists. The turnover in Paris is not even close to the same, so you can often find a favorite spot and return to it a decade later. In the age of Instagram, places go on the international radar very quickly, and though there's nothing wrong with going to an internationally known place, there's something very comforting and Parisian about finding a hole in the wall that nobody knows about but that ends up exceeding your expectations. I truly, truly do not even know the names of the places in Paris where I've had the best omelet or the best *mousse au chocolat* or the best *cassoulet*; I just stumbled upon them and discovered them and then went about my life.

When wandering into a totally random place, you could get the worst food and service—or worse, mediocre food and service, because then there's no story. At least with a really bad meal or a crazy waiter, you have an experience. But with mediocre food, it's like it didn't even exist.

But in Paris, apart from the tourist hotspots, this rarely happens. What is an average bistro experience in Paris for Parisians can be a mind-blowingly good, I-will-remember-this-forever kind of thing for Americans. Just remember to have an open mind and lots of patience, especially if you're trying to order in English and not French. Do a little recon before your trip and learn the names of a few classic dishes that you know you'll like, and then go hopping around Paris trying to find the best versions of those things. Never underestimate that cute little café down the street from your hotel even though you've never heard of it. As long as it seems relatively busy and doesn't have English menus posted outside, chances are that you'll have a good time. Here's the thing with places to eat in Paris: yes, the food is good, but the people-watching is even better.

Most often, if you go to a place that your American friend recommended, you're really only going to see other Americans enjoying Parisian food in Paris. Why not instead take nobody's recommendation but locate a cool little street, find a bistro that's busy with locals, and try to get a table? Regardless of whether your food is good or not, your experience will be fantastic. The real deal. That's what you came to Paris for, right? To see Paris and the Parisians in their natural habitat. They're not hanging out at L'Ami Louis.

Plus, if your instincts are on point and the place is packed with Parisians, I'll bet your food is fantastic. No need to map it or Instagram it or photograph it; just live it. Eat, breathe, talk, and watch everything and everyone around you. If you learn to master this (whether on a trip or in your own day-to-day life), you will experience something that Parisians have enjoyed for hundreds of years.

Seventeenth-century Paris offered an unparalleled cornucopia of cultural delights. Parisians and visitors went out to the theater and the opera, and they even went out just to be out and about. Even Parisians from the upper classes started strolling about the city—instead of always hiding away in carriages—thus providing the lower and middle classes an opportunity to observe details of their clothing, hairstyles, and mannerisms up close for the first time. According to noted French historian and author Joan DeJean,

> The most widely accessible new pleasure was one that has ever since been associated with Paris, that of simply walking its streets. With the first modern streets, the first modern bridge, and the first modern city square, Paris became the prototype for the walking city, a place where people walked not merely to get around, but by choice and for pleasure.[27]

Whether or not you go to Paris, just give this a try at home or anywhere else in the world: do nothing, but see everything. Do not make an itinerary but instead make a mental or physical shopping list of possibilities. Your time is valuable, after all. So valuable that maybe the most precious experience of all might be simply stopping and watching. Sometimes on vacation, there's no need to make reservations but just ideas of reservations, in case all else fails. If that vacation happens to be in Paris, make a reservation with yourself. Walk around, see what you see, wander into a place that looks promising, and give it a try. You might just find the best hole-in-the-wall meal that you've ever had.

France was always a country full of people-watching, but in recent years, it has been watching the world go by in a different sense. The "not about going from Point A to Point B" thing can take its toll in our fast-paced, competitive world that's dominated by speed and efficiency. France is a fantastic place for *joie de vivre* but not so much for actually making a living or accomplishing anything professionally.

As longtime Paris resident and American expat Elaine Sciolino puts it,

France today is stuck between two options, both of which are flawed. One is to embrace the tenets of a globalized world that demands technological advancement, physical mobility, and psychological fluidity. But that would run counter to traditional culture. The other is to celebrate and promote the attractive, seductive tools that worked for France in the past. But they are rusting with age and running less smoothly...There is an admiration for history and a reveling in past glory, but these are coupled with a fear of the unknown and a determination to maintain the status quo...The French know that they must find a balance between modernization (to avoid economic decline) and preservation (to avoid cultural annihilation).[28]

It's heavy stuff. I'm not sure how, or if, the French can change their rigid ways and become a force to be reckoned with in the global marketplace, but I do know that France is a great—if not the best—place to visit. While we're at it, let's discuss all of this at a Parisian café, where the traditions of pondering life's questions and watching the world go by are still alive and well.

Chapter 10

Café Society

Other than the Eiffel Tower, or perhaps a mustachioed man wearing a beret and a striped shirt while carrying a baguette, there are few things that we immediately associate with France more quickly than the image of café life.

From the beginning, cafés held an important place in society beyond just being a place to see and be seen. They were places to exchange ideas and get news that was more reliable than the newspapers provided at the time. And, of course, they were places to gossip, which is still an integral part of French life today. Long before the age of mobile phones, a Parisian's favorite one became like a phone number or address of sorts, a way to track down friends and acquaintances.

While *salons* in private homes were also places to exchange ideas (and, though rare and not nearly as influential, some are still around in Paris today), they were often more for the privileged set.

The average Parisian who wanted to discuss politics or everyday life was more likely to do so at a café. This was particularly true for those with leftist leanings, leading to the left-bank scene of the existentialists and the *soixante-huitards*, those who were a part of the civil uprisings in Paris in May 1968. Though not an official revolution, it was a social one, and it still has a great impact on life in France today. While the movement was definitely student-led, the progressive ideas espoused in *rive gauche* life played a role in expanding it into a national—and international—outcry against capitalism and traditional values.

Ironically, what was once the breeding ground for hatred of the bourgeois lifestyle is now a hotbed of the bourgeois lifestyle in Paris. The Saint-Germain-des-Prés and Café de Flore scene is moneyed and monotonous, relative to its illustrious past. That's not to say it's bad; I love it. It's just not full of creative beatnik types anymore because they've migrated north and east. There's a time and place for everything. I think there's really no better place for a tourist or an expat than this *quartier* because it's at once comforting and yet still slightly uncomfortable, which is what so many travelers want with a "foreign" experience. Just the right amount of foreign, but not too much.

Saint-Germain-des-Prés is also home to the Procope, the oldest restaurant in Paris in continuous operation. Opened in 1686, it has played meeting place or home away from home to everyone from Voltaire to Benjamin Franklin to George Sand. It is still around today, but it's not something I'd recommend visiting because it's now basically a themed museum-restaurant that's exclusively for tourists. But it is fun to note when passing by on Rue de l'Ancienne Comédie.

Coffee was first served in France in private homes in the 1640s, when beans were brought back from the Orient as souvenirs. Word about coffee spread, and by the 1660s, it was found in two kinds of Parisian homes, those of merchants who traded with the Orient and those of a select few who imported Italian chefs to oversee making it. At the time, it was approximately $4,000 for a pound of beans (in today's dollars). In 1669, when a Turkish ambassador went to stay in Paris for a year, he became the toast of the town, hosting receptions for aristocratic women in which coffee was served with great fanfare. After his departure, society ladies began to serve this trendy new beverage to their guests, and the city's love affair with coffee began. When espressos and lattes popped up around Paris, they were quite expensive, but customers were willing to pay for the new taste sensation and for the entertainment that enjoying coffee in this atmosphere provided.[29]

These days, the one caveat of the whole thing is that the coffee itself often sucks. It's sometimes very burnt and bitter, not in an "I detect notes of bitterness" sort of way but in a "how am I going to drink this swill?" sort of way. Perhaps that is how the French learned to sit at little tables and sip espresso so slowly, because they couldn't physically bear to drink it any faster. (Meanwhile, the Italians, who have the tastiest espressos in the world, take their coffees quickly, standing at the bar, and then they head on their way.)

You can order a *noisette*, which comes with a bit of foamed milk served either on top or on the side. That really helps temper the bitterness. And a number of new Brooklyn-style coffee shops have opened in Paris in the last couple of years, so it is now actually feasible to get a good cortado or pour-over if you're insistent upon great coffee. But in France, going to a café is more about the atmosphere and the comfort of a routine. Or the possibility of making an interesting and unexpected human connection.

This ambiance is what Paris is best at. I recently popped into the Café des 2 Moulins, made famous by the film *Amélie,* and though there were plenty of tourists, the setting is still just right for a little *pause.* For one euro, you can sit on a wooden stool at the simple but stunning reflective copper-topped bar and watch as people from all over the world try to fulfill their fantasies of following in the footsteps of Amélie Poulain. It is an authentic representation of what the city really is: some native inhabitants navigating around millions of dreamers trying to capture their precious Paris moments. Stepping into 2 Moulins is like stepping onto a film set. But really, practically every Parisian café feels like that. You're immediately transported to another frame of mind. Even another era perhaps.

In 1960, there were two hundred thousand of them operating in France, but now the number has dropped to approximately forty thousand.[30] But not to worry. There are still plenty for you to choose from. No *rue* in central Paris would be complete without at least one option. Feeling tired? Lonely? Bored? Overwhelmed? Freezing? Come on in to the café; it will give you what you need, plus maybe what you didn't even know you needed.

When I arrive on a red-eye from New York, the first thing I do is go to a café, stand at the bar, and have a double espresso. I am at first desperate and haggard and cranky, longing for my fix of caffeine like the addict that I am, but once a few sips go down and the beast is tamed, I always look around and appreciate the scene. In Parisian cafés, people are civil and somewhat scripted. Life feels dignified and egalitarian. Usually there is a somewhat stocky woman with short hair or a man with a beard behind the coffee bar; they are neither welcoming nor off-putting. They can do stoic, or they can do charming. As long as you speak a little French, they can be whatever you want them to be.

One customer approaches the bar for a coffee because he wants some comforting human interaction, while another customer approaches the bar for a coffee because he's reading his paper and checking his e-mails and doesn't want to be disturbed. It can involve no conversation at all or an entire day of conversation. Pound your shot of espresso and go on with your day, or linger and stir and sip and talk. The choice is yours.

Though these places originated with the idea of serving *café* (coffee), they've turned into so much more, offering a pleasant way to spend time in between meals when you have some downtime. In terms of food, a café often offers items like salads and *croque monsieur*. It is a reliable place to get a smaller and relatively inexpensive meal. Another Parisian staple is the bistro, sometimes spelled *bistrot*. The food found here is simple but often heartier, such as *coq au vin* and *parmentier de confit de canard*, and the atmosphere can be slightly fancier (though still informal). Typically these are smaller establishments with limited hours, and often they have rotating daily menus instead of just rotating *plats du jour*.

A *brasserie* is another type of informal place to eat in Paris, and it falls somewhere between the café and the bistro. The word literally means "brewery," because originally these Alsatian establishments brewed their own beer, but today they are dependable places to find *service continu*. All-day food service is something that we take for granted in the States, but it is much more difficult to come by in Paris, which is why these places are so handy. The food is generally not as good as in a more specialized bistro or restaurant, but if you are a jet-lagged tourist, a time-sensitive parent with a toddler in tow, or just someone who doesn't want to eat during the prescribed opening hours of noon to 2:00 p.m. and 7:30 p.m. to 10:30 p.m., *service continu* can save the day.

Restaurants, on the other hand, are more formal, and I highly recommend making reservations. While Americans use the term for any sort of eating establishment, in France, it implies a more upscale dining experience that always involves multiple courses. When at a restaurant of any kind in France, plan to order an appetizer (called an *entrée*, which is confusing for Americans, but because it means "entrance" in French, it actually makes a lot of sense and leads me to wonder why we call main courses "entrances" in American English) and a main course (called *plat* or *plat principal*). If you would like to eat lighter, you can order an appetizer and then select a second appetizer and explain that you'd like it as your main course. "Restaurant" is spelled the same as in English but pronounced "rehs-toh-rhan."

So a café is where you'd go to meet up with a friend or to rest between appointments, while a bistro is like your favorite neighborhood place, perfect for a cozy dinner with close friends and family. And while you might take a beer-and-comfort-food-loving coworker to a brasserie, you'd go to a restaurant for an elegant food and wine experience, hopefully involving a little romance afterward.

Chapter 11

À Table!

Americans who are really into food inevitably end up having a lifelong relationship or at least a torrid love affair with France. The birthplace of *haute cuisine* and the home of artisanal everything, France offers a cornucopia of culinary delights to suit every budget.

In order to live, we must eat. In order to live well, we must eat well. In other countries, this is often confused with eating expensively, but in France, good food is for everyone. It is a right and a privilege, and it should also be yours. If you can afford to splurge, gourmet food is a treat, but it is by no means necessary for enjoying the pleasures of eating French food.

Many French dishes, some of which have become common for us to eat today, were once considered downright exotic on American soil. While English and German tourists have enjoyed French food for centuries, the American reverence for it didn't take off until the arrival of mass air travel in the 1960s. When American tourists returned home from Paris, they regaled friends and family with their gastronomic discoveries, and French cuisine soon found a place in a nation where culinary sophistication had never before been widely desired.[31] But many of the French classics, like *coq au vin* or *bœuf bourguignon,* are dishes that developed out of a desire to make inexpensive cuts of meat or poultry taste better. When you slowly simmer less-than-prime proteins with spices and sauces, they become tender and tasty. In French cooking, anything can be made to taste good with a little TLC.

We apply the term "rustic" to simple, inexpensive dishes from the countryside, and often those very dishes end up becoming the most comforting and pleasing to eat. In addition to slow-cooked stews and roasts, one of the highlights of life in France is the ritual of regularly stopping for food at little specialty stores or markets filled with fresh produce and letting the shopping guide the cooking. Instead of stocking up on prepackaged items at big supermarkets, many French people buy only what they need and buy the best quality they can afford, which in turn makes cooking a breeze. In France, it's easy to enjoy the little luxuries, like a triple-cream cheese served at just the right temperature or a *boule* of freshly baked bread.

But you don't need to become an expat in order to enjoy the French way of eating. It's all about taking the time to make delicious dishes and to really enjoy them. Just like fashion designers who get bored with the scene often adopt a uniform of all black or jeans and white T-shirts, those at the highest echelons of the food world constantly return to the basics. Whether that means developing an interest in foraging or seeking out authentic recipes from the countryside, top chefs and epicures always seem to move past the fancy stuff and idolize the home cooking of grandmas around the world.

Plus, in reality, eating ten-course meals at Michelin-starred restaurants regularly just makes you fat. Simple but good food makes you healthy and happy. Eating well—and focusing on what you eat—helps you develop an appreciation for food, turning it into a daily pleasure that changes your quality of life in every aspect. It's good for mind, body, and heart.

The one instance in which I wholeheartedly agree with the particularly Parisian mind-set of moderation is when it comes to eating. Around age twelve, I developed a very unhealthy hate/hate relationship with my body and love/hate relationship with food. Everything was extreme. One week of indulging meant weeks of dieting and self-loathing. Either I obsessed about my body and saw food as torture and temptation to be avoided, or I stopped caring about my body and happily packed on the pounds by eating with reckless abandon. Once I gained the pounds, I unhappily went back to losing them via whatever means necessary. It was a pathetic and depressing cycle that I could not break.

Then one week, at age twenty-six, I read *The Fat Fallacy: The French Diet Secrets to Permanent Weight Loss* by Dr. Will Clower and *French Women Don't Get Fat* by Mireille Guiliano, which quite literally changed my entire relationship with food. I remember the revelation very clearly. These books gave me hope and a completely new perspective that was in contrast to my upbringing (meat-free and guilt-filled, in case you were wondering). When I picture that week now, I see myself as a wide-eyed cartoon character with a little thought bubble coming out of my head: "You mean I can eat butter and not feel bad about it?"

Since then, I haven't struggled with my weight. There are no more extreme yo-yos of gaining and losing. There's no more dieting. I used to view fat as the enemy, whereas now it is a source of pleasure, just one not to be eaten with reckless abandon. The Parisian principles of eating—put simply, eat what you want in moderation—do work, but applying American principles of eating to French food does not work.

Often when I'm around an American girlfriend who's trying to lose weight or maintain a certain weight, I notice that she cuts out things. Maybe she's avoiding anything high in fat or calories or avoiding dessert or going on a full-on diet. When I'm around a Parisienne girlfriend who's trying to lose weight or maintain a certain weight, she cuts down on portion sizes instead of cutting out things entirely. And because I truly, madly, deeply love food, the latter is something that I can get behind. Any "diet" that still allows me to eat bone marrow or foie gras or anything that I want, albeit in small portions, is something that I can actually stick with.

By observing Parisienne friends and acquaintances, I learned to order two starters instead of a starter and a main course, and I learned that it's totally okay not to finish everything on my plate, even though people will always try to make me feel like it's not okay. I learned to not let it faze me when the server inevitably asks if I didn't like something, even if I've eaten all but one or two bites of it. I learned that what I put in my body is up to me and nobody else. If I want to finish something, I finish it; if I don't want to finish something, I don't finish it.

I feel free to have a macaron whenever I want (more like two or three, because one just seems like a tease); I just don't have ten in one sitting. If I have a moment of weakness and accidentally eat too many, no problem! I don't feel guilty about it; I enjoy the experience and create a delicious food memory. But then I will have a nice salad for dinner that evening, not a three-course meal.

I learned that we can have our cake and eat it too, just perhaps not the whole cake. There's no need to count calories per se, but there is a need to make calories count. Never eat something unless you enjoy eating it, except of course when you're trying something new (or being polite). Delicious treats are special and should be savored, as should fresh fruits and vegetables and high-quality proteins. Shifting to this way of eating sounds so simple, and though it's not at first, over the years it becomes second nature. I try not to feel guilty about anything, but I make sure to have the discipline to compensate accordingly when needed.

Of course, everybody is different, and we all have our own ideal body weight, so only you can decide what is right for you. Go with whatever you think is healthy and makes you feel good. That is the beauty of the Parisian approach: you become both the watchdog and the champion of your own body. You can develop lifelong habits now that will keep you happy, satisfied, and healthy. And most of all, if you don't already, always find pleasure in food. I always remind my daughter to slow down and "savor the flavor" and enjoy every bite, and when I forget and start chowing down, she reminds me to do the same.

For me, the easiest way to slow down is to have two smaller courses instead of one plate piled with food, even if I'm eating at home. Portion sizes are important, and Texas-sized ones can make eating healthy a challenge. Another hiccup that we experience in the United States is that sugar (often in processed form) is hidden in basically everything, and sugar equals calories. Sugar and calories are fine, but not if you don't know that you're consuming them. My husband lost a lot of weight after moving to France, not by trying to, but by default through eating Parisian food the Parisian way. Considering he used to work out once or twice per day in California, exercise was not the change. The food was.

Prior to our move, we thought we were eating in a healthy way by doing most of our shopping at Whole Foods, but we later figured out that it involves so much more than that. During our time living in France, my family and I learned that when eating out or cooking at home, simple dishes are best. Paying attention to portion sizes is crucial for long-term health success. When grocery shopping, go often and buy what's whole, fresh, local, organic, and seasonal whenever possible. It sounds complicated, but buying a few fresh things every day or every other day is actually easier and cheaper than buying a grocery cart full of packaged and processed organic items once per week.

The food we eat is very important because it nourishes us and makes us feel healthy and happy, when done right. It is an important part of culture because it bonds communities. As Jean Anthelme Brillat-Savarin famously declared, "Tell me what you eat, and I will tell you what you are."

Cheese

Fromage is one of life's greatest pleasures. It can really enhance a meal, adding an interesting texture and a savory taste that just rounds everything out. Or it can be a meal (or dessert) on its own. Every good cheese offers a long-lasting, satisfying finish.

Perhaps I love it so much because I wasn't supposed to eat it growing up. When I was in elementary school, my parents started phasing out red meat and then poultry and then fish. I remember one of my favorite meals was a dish with chicken and mushrooms that my mother used to make, but that went away. My all-time favorite thing to eat as a kid was pepperoni pizza with extra pepperoni. I remember the first time I picked off all those delicious, glistening red slices at a slumber party in sixth grade. I sadly offered them to a friend, not because I wanted to, but because I felt like I had to.

Soon after, I was picking the cheese off of my pizza, trying to slyly cover it with a napkin or slide it off into the trash, because my parents had phased out dairy and insisted that I did too. That was the hardest part of all, because I *love cheese*. I didn't eat it for years, and I didn't eat anything that walked, swam, or flew (my father's definition) for about a decade. Then when I was twenty-one, a boyfriend named Giovanni came along and made me the most delicious home-cooked, meat-filled meal. He coaxed me into trying it. I did, and I never looked back. Giovanni didn't last, but my love affair with good Italian meats had just begun.

During the years when we did have dairy in the house growing up, much of it was fake, chemical-laden bright-orange cheese that came in powdered (in Kraft mac and cheese), spray can (on Triscuits, of course), or plastic-wrapped "American singles" form. It was often cooked with a fat-free, calorie-free product called I Can't Believe It's Not Butter Spray. (If you don't know what this is, Google "Fabio" and "I Can't Believe It's Not Butter Spray." I promise it will be worth it. Who says fantasies don't come true?)

I can't believe that I considered all this stuff to be actual food, but hey, we've got to start somewhere. It takes time, numerous attempts, and often just the right setting to appreciate a new food. Now my favorite cheeses come from Corsica, the smellier and stronger, the better. The transformation, as you can imagine, did not happen overnight. Époisses, for example, is an extremely pungent cheese that often stumps people the first few times but then can become a favorite, and it is widely available outside of France. I had it recently melted on a burger at Spruce in San Francisco, and wow, was it good served that way. If you haven't tried it yet, perhaps an outdoor barbecue is the best place to start. Who knows, over time, you might begin to crave it and start eating it straight out of its wooden box with a spoon or a crusty baguette.

Just like wine, a good cheese should have complexity of flavor that represents the place it comes from. What sort of grass the animals eat and how the cheese is aged or treated determine the ultimate flavor. Époisses comes from—that's right—Époisses, which is a village in Burgundy located between Dijon and Auxerre. It's a very bold cow's milk cheese that is washed in local *marc*, a liquor that is distilled from the leftovers of winemaking.

If that sounds too strong for you, the cheese named in honor of Brillat-Savarin might be just the thing. It is divine. This triple-cream (meaning it contains 75 percent or more butterfat) cow's milk Brie is produced in Burgundy and Normandy, and it's one of my go-to crowd pleasers because it's simple but still complex. It will be a hit with people who don't have much experience with French cheeses, because it tastes of salty butter and rich cream, and who doesn't like that? But if served at the right temperature, it's also pleasing to people who are really into cheese, because they'll remember just how luscious it is as it transforms in their mouths from butter and cream to hazelnuts and mushrooms. It's also fantastic served with everything from crackers to fruit to just Champagne. It checks a lot of boxes on a cheese plate and works as an appetizer, dessert, or predessert (or lunch with a nice green salad).

The actual number of different types of French cheeses is one of the great mysteries of life, like disappearing socks or men's inability to remember to put down the toilet seat. While no one can seem to agree on even a ballpark figure, everyone agrees that the cheeses of France are numerous and plentiful. This means that there is a seemingly never-ending supply of new flavors for you to try, so take advantage of France's bounty. The United States has strict laws in place for unpasteurized foods, so if you're eating French cheese here, you're not getting the real deal. Yes, it's still good—tasty cheese is tasty anywhere—but if you do go to France, make sure to take advantage of the unpasteurized *lait cru* situation. (Just make sure not to touch the cheese when in a *fromagerie*; it's a big no-no.)

Cheese experts have a lot of opinions on how to choose your cheese, but I say choose whatever calls out to you. Once you find a few that you love, challenge yourself to find a few more, and so on. If you're making a regular effort to try new ones, then the way you choose your cheese is really not that important as long as it's real cheese from a reputable market. What is important, though, is serving temperature. Americans tend to serve cheese way, way too cold. Even some good restaurants make this mistake. If your kitchen is at a normal room temperature, pull the cheese out of the fridge about two hours before serving, and it should be good to go. This makes a huge difference. Kind of like the way ice cream is not good when melted, cheese is not good when cold.

If you're putting together a cheese plate, a classic way to go is to have one goat's milk cheese, one cow's milk, and one sheep's milk. If you're entertaining, it's always a good idea to have one that's mild to please a variety of palates, and then you can experiment with the sharpness and barnyardy-ness of the others. Three cheeses work well for a small group, and five for a larger party. Playing with textures is nice too, so you can pick one that's really soft or almost runny, one that's hard, and then something in the middle to bridge the gap. When you serve them, soft cheeses should be oozing, and medium cheeses should be pillow-like to the touch.

A common inclusion on cheese plates is a bold blue. Roquefort, Fourme d'Ambert, Saint Agur, and Bleu d'Auvergne are common choices that are widely available. Saint Agur is my favorite; it's a cow's milk cheese that contains 60 percent butterfat, making it the best of both worlds between a blue and a Brie. Roquefort makers made the first attempts at securing legal protection for a food product in France. In the 1400s, they got an official monopoly on making the cheese, as declared by Charles VI, but imposter Roqueforts were still appearing centuries later. This struggle eventually led to the government protection that evolved into the system of AOC, or *Appellation d'Origine Contrôlée*, which is a certification recognizing a product's origin that is granted to certain items in France, such as butter, lentils, meat, and honey.

I enjoyed some Roquefort the other night and was transported back to an evening long before my single-girl-does-Paris trip. I had thrown on a travel show about France that I'd recorded (these were the days of TiVo), and in lieu of a typical dinner, I enjoyed a small wedge of Roquefort with some baguette and a half bottle of Champagne. It was a huge splurge for me at the time, but obviously it was worth it, because I still remember it fondly today. Curled up on my sofa in California, I felt fabulous and indulgent. I might have been far away from Paris, but I was happy as can be with my impromptu faux French trip. That's the beautiful thing about food and wine; it can serve as a link to other cultures and foster travel of the mind like nothing else can.

Bread

The origins of two of the most seemingly French things of France—croissants and baguettes—are much debated. While historians can't seem to agree upon whether or not these iconic baked goods are indeed authentically and traditionally French, there is no doubt in anyone's mind that bread in general is deeply embedded in the country's cultural identity.

The collective French mentality strongly emphasizes the protection of the working class, and bread is directly tied to this because it was historically such a major part of the everyday diet. In the eighteenth century, the average worker spent half of his daily wage on bread. When bread prices went up because of two years of failed grain crops, famine—and political turmoil—was inevitable.[32] Bread was not the sole cause of the Revolution, but it was inextricably linked to it.

The Revolution was certainly French; croissants, not so much. A crescent-shaped baked good called a kipfel dates back in Vienna to the 1200s, and moon-shaped breads in general date back even earlier. *Croissant* is the French word for crescent.

Many historians and food writers agree that the precursors to croissants as we know them today first appeared in France thanks to an Austrian. When August Zang opened a Viennese bakery in Paris in 1838, his Viennese bread and kipfels became very popular, in part because of his patented steam oven. By 1840 there were at least a dozen different makers of this type of Viennese bread.[33] The innovation of the puffed-pastry version of the kipfel occurred in

France, but since it was Austrian, which country gets credit? Either way, today there are few things more emblematic of Parisian life than a warm, buttery croissant and its aftermath of crispy fallen flakes.

But one of those things is the baguette. I find it interesting that something so powerfully symbolic is a relatively recent addition to the culinary landscape, the so-called baguette not appearing among the French breads of the nineteenth century. I even read an entire book about its history (Jim Chevallier's *About the Baguette: Exploring the Origin of a French National Icon*), and the only conclusion was really that there is no conclusion.

So no one can definitively say where the baguette originated or exactly why the baguette—as opposed to other types of long bread loaves—has become so emblematic of French culture in the last century. Why not those delicious round *boules*? *Boule*, as in *boulangerie*? But we can say that baguettes have become an important part of daily life in France, regardless of reason. We can also say that you should probably avoid getting into any arguments about the origins of French baked goods with an Austrian, in the same way that one avoids using the term "french fries" in front of a Belgian.

Baguette is the French word for a sticklike object (e.g., a wand, drumstick, or chopstick), so at least it's clear where the name comes from. And the ingredients are clear: wheat flour, water, yeast, and salt. The state of French baguettes went into a bit of a slump at one point, but now they're back, and high-quality, all natural, artisanal baguettes can be found all over France (and even all over the world). In 1993 the French government created the official designation of "the bread of French tradition." This means no additives, improvers, or technological help, and no freezing during the fermentation process.[34]

Sandwiches made from half baguettes or mini baguettes are everywhere. The most traditional kind seems to be *jambon beurre* (ham and butter), but there are numerous combinations of meats and cheeses and other things that can be had on a baguette on just about every corner in Paris. Another popular Parisian daytime staple is a *tartine*, which really just translates to a slice of bread with one or more things on top. (But doesn't the French word sound so much better?) And the ultimate *tartine* is made using Poilâne bread.

Founded in 1932 by a man named Pierre, who came to Paris from Normandy and set up shop on the Rue du Cherche-Midi in the sixth arrondissement, the Poilâne company now produces approximately 3 percent of all the bread sold in Paris. The famous *pain Poilâne*, a.k.a. *miche*, a.k.a. *pain au levain*, a.k.a. country bread, is made from stone-ground gray flour, water, and salt, and is topped with a signature *P*. In 1973, at age twenty-eight, Pierre's son Lionel began to run the company after Pierre had a stroke, and in 2002, at age eighteen, Lionel's daughter Apollonia took over as CEO after Lionel was killed in a helicopter crash. Bread is in their blood. Their *pain* is regarded in high esteem around the world, in part because of Lionel, who cultivated a global network of retailers. He was also no stranger to doing strange things for publicity, such as making a bedroom entirely out of dough for Salvador Dalí, who apparently wanted to see if he had mice.[35]

No doubt it is thanks to Lionel that I became addicted to the company's *miche* in the United States, even before I lived in Paris. Many specialty grocery stores, even as far away as California, carry the company's famous sliced bread. Poilane. com is a supercute virtual *boulangerie* where addicts can order the bread via FedEx overnight, shipped directly from the company's bakery in Paris.

Omelet

In America, omelets are standard breakfast or brunch fare, but not so in France, where they're saved mostly for lunch. But the French are on to something, because an omelet served with a green salad is light, easy, and satisfying. If you had a big lunch and aren't super-hungry at dinnertime, this is an ideal meal. Add in some goat cheese and fresh green herbs or whatever you'd like. *Frites* often accompany the omelet in cafés and brasseries, but you can always ask for a *salade verte* instead. Or have a little of both because it's a tasty combination.

Crêpes

A common offering from street vendors in Paris, crêpes are the ideal hot treat for cold days. They are also one of the few food items that are culturally acceptable to eat on the street if you are standing near the street vendor where you bought them.

The buckwheat version, galettes, have been a specialty of the Bretagne (Brittany) region of France for centuries. Duchess Anne of Bretagne planted buckwheat in the region during the fifteenth century because it was a nutritious plant that grew easily and quickly in the region's poor soil.[36]

My favorite buckwheat galette can be found on Sundays at the organic farmers' market on Boulevard Raspail in the sixth arrondissement; it's open in the morning until about 1:00 p.m. or so. There's a stall that offers freshly made ones with a slice of ham, a little cheese, a fresh egg, and a healthy dash of black pepper. It's the perfect breakfast to enjoy while walking around the market and doing a little shopping (or people-watching and food ogling).

Soufflé

Soufflés are most definitely French in origin, dating back to the eighteenth century. Because they are so hard to get just right, they are really best left up to the professionals, in my opinion. They just involve so much pressure. There's a restaurant (appropriately named Le Soufflé) on Rue Mont-Thabor in the first arrondissement of Paris that offers an entire prix fixe menu of soufflés, so you can eat a starter, main course, and dessert entirely of the French specialty, with a *salade verte* thrown in for good measure. If you're a fan and you're headed to Paris, make sure to check it out.

Croque Monsieur

A *croque monsieur* is a baked sandwich comprising ham, cheese, and a buttery *béchamel* sauce. It is also available with a fried egg on top, which creates a *croque madame.* The sandwich actually originated in Wales. The first official recognition of cheese on toast appears in Auguste Escoffier's culinary bible, *Le Guide Culinaire*, in 1903, in which he describes it as Welsh rarebit.[37] These days it's a popular lunchtime dish in Paris.

Salade Verte

A *salade verte* is just a green salad, but in France, it can actually be exciting. The best ones are composed of bright-green mâche, pale-green butter lettuce, nearly white frisée, and purple-and-white-striped radicchio. The salad will be topped with the establishment's vinaigrette of choice. If you're in a run-of-the-mill café in Paris, this will probably be bottled vinaigrette and might even be a bit artificially sweet, which is a shame. A great Parisian vinaigrette should be whisked by hand and should comprise Dijon mustard, sunflower oil, salt, pepper, red wine vinegar, chopped garlic or shallots, and chopped fresh herbs. In the South of France, olive oil replaces the sunflower oil, and fresh lemon juice replaces the vinegar.

I grew up eating mostly ranch dressing, always requiring a heavy dosage of some sort of salad dressing in order to be able to eat lettuce. But that all changed over a meal in Avignon, where I completely freaked out over a simple green salad. It was just so good, and it was only lettuce, olive oil, and salt. That's it. But the lettuce was a beautiful bounty of all different types of fresh, delicate, and tender leaves, and the extra-virgin olive oil was a powerful one from Provence.

The thick and cloudy oil was also poured into little dishes to use as a dip for bread, which is how we noticed that it was as green as freshly cut grass, and the taste made us almost feel like coughing as it coated our throats. Far from being a lowly cooking aid, it added a depth of flavor and a textural mouthfeel that transformed everything we put it on. It was light years away from that thin, flaccid yellow stuff that's often plopped down on American restaurant tables (alongside balsamic vinegar, table salt, and pepper that looks more like miniature gray confetti than freshly ground peppercorns).

And I can't forget to tell you about the salt, because that is really the icing on the proverbial cake. This salad in Avignon—and every salad that I've made since—was topped with truly good-quality salt, the kind that makes you wonder how you ever found those glass shakers of table salt with their grains of rice and dirty, dented silver tops appealing. In the case of the salad in Avignon, the salt took the form of little crunchy crystals of *fleur de sel,* which is hand-harvested by workers who scrape off the top layer of salt from the sea before it sinks to the bottom of large salt pans. Yum.

So below is my recipe for the best side salad ever. Thanks, Avignon.

Salade Verte

Prep time: Takes seconds to make
Serves as few or as many people as you'd like

fresh organic lettuce (preferably a mix of a few different types that you enjoy)
the best-quality extra-virgin olive oil that you can find
a pinch of *fleur de sel* or some other delicious sea salt from your local market

Put the lettuce in a bowl, drizzle on a healthy amount of olive oil, sprinkle with salt, toss, and serve immediately.

Chèvre Chaud

Everyone—tourists and Parisians—seems to love *le chèvre chaud*, or warm goat cheese salad. Consisting of goat cheese melted on toast, a green salad with vinaigrette, and the occasional tomato wedge, it is a wildly popular dish that feels light but also satisfying. You can sometimes get away with ordering just that if it's for lunch, but at dinnertime, it's always served as an appetizer.

Steak Tartare

Le tartare de bœuf is perfect for enjoying in a restaurant, but it's not really something I'd encourage you to try making at home because the primary ingredient is raw beef. There are many variations, but a classic version might mix the chopped raw beef with capers, chives or parsley, shallots, Dijon mustard, egg yolk, olive oil, salt, and pepper. It's delicious.

Steak Frites

The most classic Parisian meal for locals and tourists is probably *steak frites* (steak with fries). It's everywhere, it's tasty, and it's easy to order.

Steak, and beef dishes in general, did not originally come from the region but from England. Occupying English troops brought steak to France sometime after the Battle of Waterloo in 1815. The word "steak" comes from England, derived from "steikjo," which means "to roast" in Old Norse.[38] I don't know if Parisians would appreciate this fun fact very much, but there you have it. French fries don't come from France either; they are actually from Belgium. The French and Belgians are still quarreling about this one, but I've got to side with the Belgians after reviewing the evidence.

When eating *frites*, try to forgo the ketchup and dip them into Dijon or mayonnaise, or enjoy them plain. They really don't need the ketchup. In addition, note that it is considered polite to eat them with a fork instead of with your hands.

Poulet Rôti

Roast chicken can be found pretty much everywhere in France. When walking down a market street, you're guaranteed to see a place with a large, warm, aromatic rotisserie filled with glistening golden-brown chickens rotating on metal rods, their juices dripping and skins crackling. Buy one and some good lettuce, and you're set for lunch or dinner.

If you'd like to make it at home, you don't need a rotisserie, just your oven. The most important thing is to buy the best chicken that you can find (free-range, hormone-free, etc.) from a good butcher or your favorite trusted market. I have the butcher remove the insides for me because I'm kind of a wimp. Below is my favorite way to make it.

Roasted Chicken

Prep/cook time: 1½ hours
Serves 2–4, depending on portion sizes

1 whole chicken, 3–4 pounds
1 head of garlic
½ stick European or European-style butter (either salted or unsalted)
fresh thyme
fine sea salt
freshly ground black pepper

Preheat the oven to 350 degrees (Fahrenheit).
Place the whole chicken into an oval baking dish. Cut off the top ¼ of a head of garlic, revealing the insides of the cloves but

leaving them in their skins. Nestle the garlic into the baking dish with the chicken. Cut up the butter into little cubes, place them all over the chicken, and then generously salt the whole thing with fine sea salt. Add in fresh thyme sprigs; this doesn't have to be exact, but I usually add about fifteen sprigs sort of haphazardly all over the pan.

Bake the chicken for 1 hour and 25 minutes. Thirty minutes into the baking, remove the chicken, and rotate it and the head of garlic upside down. Do this again after another 30 minutes of baking to return it to its original upright position. The top should be nicely golden brown; if you see it getting too dark during the second rotation, turn down the oven's temperature slightly.

Transfer the chicken and head of garlic to a serving dish, and discard the thyme and butter remains. Add some additional fresh uncooked thyme to the dish if you'd like (it smells great). Season with plenty of pepper before serving.

Sole Meunière

Sole has been a staple of elegant French dining for centuries, but it wasn't widely known in the United States until Julia Child freaked out when she first tasted *sole meunière*. (Later Meryl Streep recreated this moment while playing Julia Child in the film *Julie & Julia*.)

The version I make at home has a lot less butter than those in Paris, but it still feels rich and satisfying. Traditionally, it is served with a brown butter sauce over the top, but I like to substitute olive oil for this part. I know that sounds crazy, but there's already a coating of brown butter in the pan from cooking the fish, and the combination of butter and olive oil is quite nice.

Simple *Sole Meunière*

Prep/cook time: 20 minutes
Serves 4

4 fillets of wild sole, 4–5 ounces each (make sure the fish is wild and not farmed if possible, and ask your fishmonger to remove the skin and pin bones)

2 tablespoons all-purpose flour (Cup4Cup flour works here if you want to make it gluten-free)

½ teaspoon good-quality fine salt

freshly ground black pepper

4 tablespoons salted butter

2 tablespoons olive oil

2 tablespoons freshly squeezed lemon juice (plus lemon wedges for serving)

1 tablespoon finely chopped flat-leaf parsley

Wash the sole fillets with cold water and pat completely dry. Mix the flour, salt, and pepper in a shallow baking dish and coat the fish, making sure there is a light dusting over every part of each fillet. Place a large pan on medium-high heat, wait a minute or two until it's hot, and melt half (2 tablespoons) of the butter. Add two of the fillets to the pan, cook about 3 minutes on one side (or until lightly browned), and then flip and cook on the other side for 3 minutes. Remove the fillets from the pan and place them on a clean plate. Add the other 2 tablespoons of butter and repeat the process with the other two fillets.

Once all of the fish is cooked, turn the heat down to low and add the 2 tablespoons of olive oil to the pan. Quickly add the lemon juice and parsley and stir until combined, only about 30 seconds or so. Pour the sauce over the fish immediately. Plate the fillets and sprinkle with salt and pepper.

Serve with plenty of lemon wedges and a green salad on the side. It's nice to have a proper acidic vinaigrette on the salad to go with the fish, and you can make one ahead of time (though wait to dress the lettuce until right before serving). Whisk together a good one with Dijon mustard, lemon juice, Champagne or white wine vinegar, sea salt, freshly ground pepper, and tons of extra-virgin olive oil. Play with the proportions of the vinaigrette until you're satisfied with the balance and texture.

Moules Marinière

I had tried mussels here and there, mostly at the insistence of friends and not because I was really excited about the dish. The first time I really tackled a massive bowl of them was on my honeymoon, at a brasserie on Rue de Buci on the *rive gauche*. My husband and I had previously been removing the meat of the mussels with forks, but an elegant older French woman sitting next to us taught us how to get the meat out her way. Because a mussel shell has two sides when cooked and opened, you can break it in half, turning one half of the shell into a spoon that you can use to dig out the meat of the rest of the mussels. Yes, it's still messy, but it works so much better.

The next time we went back, we sat outside on the heated terrace, enjoying our buttery bowl of mussels with a baguette and frites, and a gentleman who was sitting next to us turned to us and asked us if we would like the rest of his bottle of wine. He was finished with his meal, and he thought his Chablis would be a much better pairing than the white wine we'd chosen. He gave us some pointers on wine pairings, signed his bill, and wished us well.

Needless to say, such kind gestures are a rarity in France, so our honeymoon experience on Rue de Buci still holds a special place in our hearts. I eventually learned how to make the dish at home, and I always serve it with a crisp Chablis.

Once in Mykonos, we had a big bowl of mussels but with feta added; it was a salty, tasty culinary epiphany. Now I make mussels regularly during fall and winter, and I've included my recipe below—feta included—for a cozy meal at home. Serve with a good baguette and a green salad.

Steamed Mussels with Feta

Prep/cook time: 45 minutes

Serves 4 as a main course with salad and bread, or 8 as an appetizer

3 pounds of mussels (I buy 3.5 pounds because I'm extremely picky and do not use any cracked or slightly opened mussels.)
extra-virgin olive oil
3 tablespoons good-quality salted butter
1 leek (white and very light green parts only), finely diced
3 garlic gloves, minced
1 cup white wine (enjoy the rest with your finished dish)
½ cup flat-leaf parsley, chopped
1 cup good-quality French or Greek feta, diced into cubes
sea salt
freshly ground pepper

Place the mussels on ice on one side of your sink. Rinse under cold water and pull off any of the beards. Note that this part can take quite a bit of time, so plan accordingly. Discard any that are cracked or opened; when in doubt, toss it out!

Heat 2 tablespoons of olive oil and 1 tablespoon of butter in a large pot (a pasta pot works well) over medium heat. Add the leeks and garlic and cook about 5 minutes, stirring frequently to make sure they don't burn. Carefully add the mussels and very carefully add in the white wine. Stir everything together. Cover and steam the mussels for 10 minutes or until the mussels open. Make sure to stir occasionally during this process.

Add the remaining 2 tablespoons of butter and a little more olive oil, plus a healthy pinch of sea salt and some freshly ground pepper. Add in the cheese and parsley, turn off the heat, and stir everything together. Serve immediately in bowls alongside a crusty baguette, bowls for the empty shells, forks, and plenty of napkins.

Confit de Canard

Duck confit and many other duck dishes are big-time staples of bistros and brasseries in Paris. Recreating this classic dish at home is easy because legs of duck confit are widely available in the United States from D'Artagnan, and they're really good. All of the hard work is done for you. They are individually wrapped (so they're good for cooking for one or two people), and they last for a long time in the fridge, so they're nice to have on hand for the next time you feel like making a fancy meal that takes all of ten minutes. All you have to do is heat up the duck confit and serve it with a salad, or with a salad and potatoes if you'd like to make it more substantial. Duck confit is salty, savory, and most definitely satisfying.

Cassoulet

This supremely comforting dish is not from Paris, but it can be found all over Paris during the colder months. A regional specialty of Southern France, cassoulet comes from the three towns of Castelnaudary, Carcassonne, and Toulouse. The dish is named after the glazed earthenware pot in which it is traditionally cooked, called a *cassole*.

Though the three towns argue over whose version is the best or most authentic—similar to heated arguments about barbecue in North Carolina, Tennessee, and Texas or about Chicago versus New York pizza or chili across the United States (except this debate goes back to the 1300s)—Castelnaudary is generally regarded as the king of cassoulet. For the sake of simplicity, let's just say that though there are many variations, a typical cassoulet might include white beans, potted duck, sausage, various cuts of pork, garlic, and herbs.

Before you begin buying ingredients, I should warn you that this is not an inexpensive dish to make, especially if you are in the States. Things like duck leg confit, bouquet garni, and the right sausage can also take a lot of time to find. But it's a great dish for holiday entertaining or for your family to enjoy a few nights in one week. Plus, it freezes well. Oh, and it's unbelievably delicious.

Cassoulet is a stick-to-your-ribs, now-it's-time-for-a-nap kind of one-pot meal. I make it every year for Christmas Eve dinner plus other times throughout the winter whenever I'm feeling like nesting. It's also great for entertaining because not only can you make it ahead but also it tastes much better that way, and it can be heated and reheated over and over without drying out.

Although making the cassoulet in two parts over the course of two days might seem laborious, it is really the only way to get that savory delicious crust on top. People who are really into food will surely be aghast that I am calling for canned white beans instead of the traditional dried Tarbais ones, but I find that the end result tastes just as good, without all of that overnight soaking business.

Another controversial thing is I've included tomatoes—and canned ones at that—which are not traditional, but I love the flavor. If you're going for authenticity, skip the tomatoes and any canned products. As long as you don't have anyone from Carcassonne or Castelnaudary coming for dinner, you should be fine.

My version is a hybrid of some of my favorite ones that I've enjoyed in France.

Cassoulet

Prep/cook time: This takes a really long time to make, but it is well worth it

Serves 8

2 cans cannellini beans, no salt added (organic if possible)

extra-virgin olive oil

2 cloves garlic, diced

2 white onions, chopped

2 carrots, chopped

freshly ground black pepper

1 pound pork shoulder; have your butcher cut into 1-inch cubes

½ pound pancetta; have your butcher dice into very small cubes

2 cups whole peeled canned tomatoes, pierced open and ever-so-slightly crushed, plus two-thirds of the juices from the can

2 bouquets garni (These are tied bundles or sachets of dried herbs, usually thyme, bay leaf, parsley, basil, rosemary, tarragon, and chervil. They are available on Amazon if not at your local market. Once I thought I had some on hand but didn't and used five dried bay leaves instead, and the cassoulet still tasted great.)

1 cup white wine (any kind will do, but pick something you like and enjoy the remainder while cooking)

2 cups low-sodium chicken broth (Pacific organic free-range chicken broth is the absolute best and makes a big difference in the outcome; in this case, it does not need to be low-sodium.)

1 cup water

4 confit duck legs (D'Artagnan makes the best outside of France.)

1 pound pork sausages (If you're in New York, try to find one large Trois Petits Cochons "Saucisson à l'Ail" from Brooklyn, available in specialty markets. If you're able to find it, cut off the tip of both ends and cut it in half; when you brown it in the pan, the casing will crackle and pop off, and you can discard it. If you can't find Trois Petits Cochons, ask your butcher for pork sausage that will be good to brown, slice, and add to a stew. Have the casings left on.)

Day 1:

Preheat the oven to 300 degrees (Fahrenheit). Rinse the beans very thoroughly in a colander and set aside. Heat 2 tablespoons of olive oil over medium-high heat in a Dutch oven (a large cast-iron pot), and lightly brown the garlic, onions, and carrots for 10 minutes, stirring often so nothing gets too browned. Remove the vegetables and set aside. Add another 2 tablespoons of olive oil into the same pot, and brown the pork shoulder and pancetta for 8 minutes after adding more pepper.

Add the garlic, onions, carrots, tomatoes with most of their juices, and beans to the pot along with the bouquets garnis. Cook until the liquid thickens, about 10 minutes. Add the wine and reduce it by half, stirring often. Add the broth and bring to a boil, and then add the cup of water. Reduce heat to medium. Cook uncovered until liquid has thickened, which should be about 30 minutes, stirring occasionally. Discard the bouquets garnis and set the pot aside, away from the heat.

Meanwhile, sear the duck confit in another tablespoon of olive oil in a large skillet or pan over medium-high heat for 8 minutes; then remove it from the heat and transfer to a plate. Brown the sausages in the duck fat for about 8 minutes. Remove from the pan and cut into ½-inch slices. Pull the duck meat off the bones and discard the fat and bones. Stir the duck confit and sausages into the cassoulet with all of the other ingredients.

Drizzle a little olive oil over the top and bake uncovered for one hour. Remove from the oven and let cool completely, stirring several times as it cools, and then put in the refrigerator overnight.

Day 2:

Preheat the oven to 300 degrees. Bake uncovered for 1 hour. Pull the cassoulet out of the oven and gently stir. Put it back into the oven, raise the oven temperature to 450 degrees, and cook the cassoulet until the top is bubbly and slightly browned, which should be about 5 or 6 minutes. Let cool for 5 to 10 minutes and then serve. Though it's not traditional, I think it's great served with a spinach salad.

Potatoes

Other than as *pommes frites* (fries), potatoes are found every-where in Parisian eating establishments, from the most casual bras-serie to Michelin-starred restaurants. Potatoes are called *pommes de terre* and can be found everywhere. Be prepared; there is a ton of butter in French mashed potatoes. That is not a bad thing, but just know that a little goes a long way.

A perennial potato favorite is the classic dish *gratin dauphinois*. It is so creamy that you'll swear there's cheese in it, but there's not. It dates back to the eighteenth century, but it is still a staple on Parisian bistro menus today.

Here is my recipe:

Gratin Dauphinois
Prep/cook time: 1 hour
Serves 8

2 pounds of potatoes (medium-sized waxy yellow ones, such as Yukon Gold, are best), sliced thin with a mandoline
2 cups whole milk
1 teaspoon salt
freshly grated nutmeg
¼ cup heavy cream
1 tablespoon chives, finely chopped

Preheat the oven to 425 degrees (Fahrenheit). Rinse the potatoes. I don't peel my potatoes, because I like the skin, but feel free to peel them if you'd like. Slice them thinly (about one-tenth of an inch); you really should use a mandoline for this. You can use a knife if you don't have one, but it will be difficult to get the slices thin enough. Also note that you should always use a safety glove of metal fabric when using a mandoline; otherwise you are pretty much guaranteed to slice the tip of one of your fingers off someday.

Place the sliced potatoes in a large saucepan with the milk, salt, and some freshly grated nutmeg. Bring to a simmer over medium heat for 8 to 10 minutes, until the milk thickens into a creamy sauce, stirring throughout. Do not let the milk scorch.

Turn off the heat and transfer the potatoes and sauce into a ceramic or glass baking dish. Pour the heavy cream evenly over the top. Bake for 35 to 40 minutes until the potatoes are slightly browned on top. Sprinkle on the chives just before serving.

Chocolate

I am hopelessly addicted to dark chocolate. I can't remember the last time I didn't have a couple of squares of a dark chocolate bar (called a *tablette* in French) before bed. If I have a dessert that consists of other flavors, I still have to have some chocolate afterward. Fruit just doesn't cut it.

Good-quality dark chocolate—not the kind with long ingredient lists, but the real stuff—is smoky, nutty, slightly sweet, and a bit spicy. And Paris is a chocolate lover's paradise. It is rare to walk more than five minutes without seeing some beautifully displayed cocoa-dusted truffles and perfectly formed bonbons in the *vitrine* of a pastry shop or chocolate shop. Or those sticky candied orange slices enrobed in a thick layer of dark chocolate, hitting just the right balance of sweet, sour, gooey, and crunchy. Mmm. Now that's a fruit dessert that counts.

Other than tablettes, bonbons, truffles, and candied fruits covered in chocolate, a great way to get your chocolate fix at home is via *mousse au chocolat*. Here is my version:

Mousse au Chocolat

Prep/cook time: 30 minutes, plus 4 hours of cooling time
Serves 8
The mousse is prettiest served in white ramekins, which you can find on Amazon or at any kitchen store. Ramekins are very handy to

have, and not just for this recipe. You can use them for prepping, cooking, snacking, or serving in a variety of ways. They can go in the oven, fridge, or dishwasher, so don't hesitate to buy a set.

8 ounces of dark chocolate chips (I use Guittard extra-dark chocolate baking chips, 63 percent cacao; these come in 11.5-ounce bags, and it's fine to guesstimate the 8 ounces.)
6 tablespoons of salted butter
6 large eggs (yolks and whites separated)
¼ cup plus 3 tablespoons white sugar

Separate your egg yolks and egg whites, prep all ingredients, and pull out your electric mixer. Put around one inch of water in the bottom of a *bain marie* or double boiler (or just a smaller pot over a larger pot), and place on the stovetop on medium heat. Add the chocolate chips and butter and melt, stirring occasionally. Once the chocolate and butter are totally melted and mixed, remove from heat and set aside.

Beat the egg yolks and ¼ cup of sugar in an electric mixer for 5 minutes. Pour the yolks into a clean bowl and set aside. Clean the electric mixer and its bowl, and beat the egg whites and 3 tablespoons of sugar for 5 minutes. Remove the egg-white bowl from the electric mixer and set aside.

Gently fold the egg-yolk mixture into the melted chocolate with a spatula, stirring constantly until completely combined. Take that mixture and gently fold it into the egg-white mixture, a little at a time, until completely combined and no white streaks remain. Divide the mixture into 8 ramekins, cleaning off any spills as you go. Shake each ramekin very gently to settle the surface, and smooth if necessary. Chill in the fridge for 4 hours.

Note: One of the best things about this recipe is that even though it does take time and effort to make, you can make them days in advance, so they're great for entertaining. Alternatively, you can save them for yourself and enjoy them eight nights in a row. Do not try to cut the recipe in half. I tried that once, and the electric mixer doesn't have enough eggs to reach and beat, so the whole thing comes out completely different and not nearly as light and fluffy.

Another delicious way to get your chocolate fix is through a *gâteau moelleux*, called molten chocolate cake or lava cake in the United States. Made from butter, sugar, chocolate, and eggs, this brownie-like cake with a gooey chocolatey center is available as dessert practically everywhere in France. Jean-Georges Vongerichten says he accidentally invented the cake in New York in 1987 when he was serving hundreds of people a chocolate cake that was mistakenly undercooked in the center. He says that he was very upset, but then the entire crowd loved the dessert so much that it became an instant hit. Jacques Torres disagrees, saying that the cake was invented in France much earlier. Whoever invented it, bravo.

Tarte Tatin

A sort of French version of an apple pie, *tarte tatin* is another staple of Parisian cafés and bistros. It is basically an upside-down apple tart baked with a buttery, flaky crust placed on top of a caramelized apple filling, which is inverted after baking. I tried making it once at home but never again. It is nowhere near as easy to make as apple pie, so I have respect for the people who are turning them out daily.

The creation of the dessert is credited to two sisters named Stéphanie (Fanny) and Caroline Tatin, who lived in a little town called Lamotte-Beuvron. In the 1880s, their apple tart became quite popular. It was then regularly served at Hotel Tatin, which the sisters opened in 1894, thus the name. The first printed mention of the *tarte tatin* was in 1903.[39] Some scholars have pointed out that upside-down tarts were a specialty of that region before the sisters started serving theirs, but everyone seems to agree that the sisters perfected the recipe, paving the way for the *tarte tatin* loved around the world today.

~

When an American goes to Paris, not only are there new dishes to encounter but also there are some new table manners and customs as well. Below is a quick primer just in case you're interested in avoiding a dining faux pas. Many of the French dining customs actually make a lot of sense and are far more chic than the typical American ones. Others, such as not cutting lettuce leaves, not so much. Skip this if you're already an international manners pro.

- Your fork always belongs in your left hand and your knife in your right hand when eating appetizers or main courses. Always. Don't switch back and forth. This one makes so much sense because it's quite silly to switch utensils between hands or to attempt to cut things with a fork.

- Your fork tines should be pointing down whenever possible. This is extremely tricky to get the hang of at first and is really not logical, but it just looks so good when done properly.

- Fold your lettuces leaves; don't cut them. I'm still getting the hang of this and find it to be nearly impossible at times, but I had to include it in case you find yourself eating with French people. Apparently the logic is that it's rude to cut your lettuce because it signals that your host or hostess (or restaurant) didn't do a good job of cutting it into proper pieces. But really, this one sucks. Having been raised in a place where chopped salads are an everyday staple, I find large lettuce leaves to be positively daunting.

- Eat fries with a fork. This one is a no-brainer because it prevents you from getting greasy fingers.

- Wait until the first course has begun to begin eating bread; the bread isn't the first course. When in France, place your bread directly on the table (even at nice restaurants). Avoid putting bread on the table upside down because that is considered to be bad luck.

- As aforementioned, make sure to order two courses when eating in a restaurant.

- Unlike in the United States, hands are supposed to go on the table when eating, not in your lap. It's actually much more comfortable and natural once you get the hang of it. Keeping my hands folded in my lap now feels stiff, so this one I take full advantage of.

- When you're finished with a course, place your fork and your knife parallel on your plate, pointing approximately to ten o'clock, never crossed.

- Never ever ask for a doggy bag, no matter how much food you have left over. This is no joke. When I lived in Paris, I knew this rule and always followed it...except for one night when I didn't. I couldn't help myself. My husband and I were obsessed with Brasserie Lutetia's *poulet fermier de Challans* (chicken roasted with fragrant garlic and thyme nestled in a bed of fluffy mashed potatoes whipped with a ton of cream and butter, all served in a black cast-iron pot), and we ordered one for each of us. We ordered our daughter the chicken from the children's menu, which turned out to be the exact same dish as ours, in the exact same size. This thing was massive. And superrich. One was enough for two people; three would be insane. Our daughter didn't even want any by the time it arrived; she was full from her first course and from bread, and she was falling asleep on the banquette. It was late, and she was only two years old. So our old American habits kicked in, and we asked if we could take her untouched chicken and mashed potatoes home with us. And just like that, a dark French cloud hovered over our table. The whole dinner changed. Our server shot us his best Parisian glare (really, it was a quite impressive one) plus a firm and uncharacteristically loud *non, absolument pas*, repeated several times for emphasis. We received the cold shoulder for the rest of the evening. Word got around to the restaurant staff, and it was definitely a *thing*. So take it from me: don't ask for a doggy bag for any reason while in Paris. Also, never underestimate a Parisian kids' menu.

- If you'd like some more wine and there's a bottle on the table, feel free to pour yourself some but only after asking if anyone else at the table would like more first.

Chapter 12

Tchin Tchin

There are few things more pleasing in life than the sound of a Champagne cork popping. *Pourquoi? Parce que* it means that something good is about to happen. What follows the popping sound is inevitably something delicious, lively, romantic, or sinful. All of the above? You lucky thing.

Champagne has a supremely glamorous past. Beginning in the year 898, all of the French kings were crowned in the Champagne region, and the beverage of the same name flowed freely at the coronation banquets. To this day, no French party is complete without Champagne. Just before turning fifty years old, Brigitte Bardot claimed that it was "the one thing that gives me zest when I feel tired."[40]

The winters in the region get very cold, and a long time ago, the cold temperatures caused wine fermentation to stop, and then it underwent a second fermentation as the weather got warmer. The result was often exploding bottles or bubbles in the wine, which the winemakers in the region (most notably a monk named Pierre Pérignon) considered to be a fault. In the eighteenth century, the version with bubbles became a hit in the royal court, and by the nineteenth century, winemakers had more or less figured out the bubble-making-and-maintaining process, and the modern Champagne industry was on track.

Today Champagne is made via the traditional *methode Champenoise* from a combination of chardonnay, pinot noir, and pinot meunier grapes (though not necessarily all in one) and can only be called Champagne if it comes from the Champagne region of France. *Blanc de blancs* is made entirely from white grapes (hence the name), and it is a no-brainer for pleasing pretty much all palates. It's crisp and fresh and a bit salty because of the region's chalky soil. *Blanc de noirs* is made from red grapes, and *rosé* from a blend of red and white grapes. If a Champagne is labeled "nonvintage," that means that it is a blend of different vintages, while "vintage" indicates that it is made from the grapes of only one year's harvest. If a label says "brut," that means it can have up to twelve grams of sugar per liter, while "extra brut" can have up to six grams and "brut nature" up to three grams. The addition of sugar (and sometimes flavors) to Champagne is called the *dosage*.

Just please don't serve prosecco and call it Champagne. Yes, they are both bubbly, but that's where the similarities end. If you prefer a drier style of wine, go with Champagne or a French sparkling wine; only choose prosecco if you enjoy wine that's light with in-your-face candied-fruit flavors and a pronounced aftertaste. (Clearly, I prefer the former.) Champagne smells and tastes more like toast and almonds, is a great match with a variety of foods, and has a much more elegant finish.

If possible, opt for grower Champagne instead of the big-name brands, and you will notice a difference. Many of the big boys (i.e., all of the "good" branded ones you see everywhere with bold labels) buy their grapes, thus emphasizing marketing over grape-growing practices. They're also meant to please the masses, so they will generally be sweeter and won't have the same finesse that grower Champagnes have. If you're looking for a more affordable alternative to Champagne—and understandably so, because it does not come cheap—sparkling wines from Bourgogne, Loire, and Jura (called *crémant*) provide scrumptiously satisfying bubbles at a fraction of the price. These sparkling wines are becoming quite popular and more widely available, so check your local wine shop or favorite online retailer.

When in France, order a glass of Champagne by saying "*une coupe*" and save *verre*, the word for "glass," for ordering a glass of wine: "*Est-ce que je peux avoir un verre de vin rouge?*"

I'm no sommelier, but I drink a lot of wine. Any good wine professional will tell you that that is the best way to learn about the subject. Drink often, pay attention to what you're drinking, and try different wines as much as possible. Learning about wine is one of the few things in life that combines study with pleasure. It's a mind-altering substance that's not only legal but also totally socially appropriate. Who knew geography and agriculture could be so entertaining?

Wine is instant gratification in a glass, offering a laundry list of immediate positive benefits. It acts as a social lubricant, a natural stress reliever, and a powerful aphrodisiac. Having just one glass can change the entire course of your evening.

Through my completely unscientific research, I can tell you that there is usually a very big difference between a couple sitting down to dinner together with no wine and a couple sitting down to dinner together with a bottle of wine. Phones are set aside a bit more, eye contact is made, and laughter is abundant. Or sometimes tears are abundant, but in those cases, it can be a good thing. When wine is present, generally things that need to be discussed are discussed.

Just think of the small talk and reserved politeness at the beginning of a party versus the witty jokes and unabashed flirting that occur only a couple of hours later. Or how you feel after leaving a stressful day at work—your shoulders one big, knotted, tense mess—versus how you feel just one hour later after enjoying a glass. Part of the beauty of meeting a friend for a drink is, well, the drink. Wine lets our guard down for us, giving us the confidence to let loose and feel good. Perhaps best of all, it offers us the clarity to stop multitasking. We can just be present in the moment.

And that's just the mediocre stuff.

A glass of really good wine forces you not only to stop multitasking but also to focus on what you are enjoying. What is the exact shade? The precise aroma? And what does it actually taste like? Suddenly wine is not just a color. It's not "I'll have the white" or "I only drink red."

As you swirl it around in your glass, you'll notice that it's yellow like pale straw or golden like the not completely molten bits of a crème brûlée. It runs thick and opaque like the ink of a fountain pen or muddled and brown like the color of a rusty nail. It smells like prickly pear or a ripened banana, like freshly ground black pepper or a newly purchased leather belt. And though it's bursting with flavor, you find it difficult to identify exactly what you taste when it first hits your tongue, even when you roll it around in your mouth in an attempt to capture every drop, and even still when it washes down your throat, perfectly cleansing your palate for another bite of food.

Good wine doesn't need to be fancy; it can be whatever suits you and makes you happy, as long as you don't drink the same varietal, producer, or style over and over. Mix it up. Cheat on your favorites, and I guarantee you'll find new ones.

I began with cases of riesling that my mother bought me from Sam's Club (like a lame version of Costco without all of the free samples). I was nineteen and home for the summer from college. It cost about four dollars per bottle, and it was like drinking honeyed nectar, and I loved every cloying drop of it. It began to accompany my evening experiments in the kitchen, and it made cooking so much more fun. Then it started to taste too sweet, so I moved on to chardonnay. Later on in life, California chardonnay became too oaky/buttery/overripened/artificial to me, so it was on to white Burgundy. And so the cycle of wine began. Now when it comes to white wine, the funkier and more obscure, the better. And few things in life make me as happy as smelling and sipping a well-balanced red Burgundy.

Everyone's journey is different, as are everyone's palate and budget, but if you get into wine, chances are that you'll end up discovering that there's something magical about the French ones. They're alive; their character comes more from the soil and the grapes than from the people making them (except when they've been Robert Parker–ed; all bets are off when the *vignerons* are into *le marketing* and homogeneity among vintages to please the masses).

In general, I think of New World wine (e.g., Californian, Chilean) as more of a man-made product, while Old World wine (e.g., French, Italian) is more of an agricultural product. It's nature versus nurture. Of course, there are many exceptions on both sides, but I think it's easier to pick really interesting wines that offer good value from the French section of the wine list.

In the New World, we're quite good at marketing and efficiency, and though these are great business skills, they do not really make for the best grape-growing and winemaking processes. In the Old World, vineyards were observed for centuries and patiently mapped out. Some areas of land were identified as making beautiful grapes (and therefore great wine), while others were identified as being more relevant for middle-of-the-road wine. These subdivisions became known as *terroirs*. Both geographical and a bit romantic, this concept is the single most important part about wine. Technically, *terroir* is what makes one vineyard different from another, but it also encompasses the soul of a vineyard.[41] *Terroir* mostly comes from the soil, but the local climate is also extremely important. And, of course, the approach of the people growing the grapes and making the wine is a major factor in the outcome. Every wine is defined by these key elements.

It's best to seek out small producers; that way you really experience the *terroir*, whereas with the big-name wine brands, you're mostly just paying for marketing. Do skip your local grocery store and find a small wine shop instead. Once you find a shop that you trust, you can learn a lot about wine and figure out what you like and don't like. Larger grocery stores and wine emporiums often carry the big-name brands of wine, and the value and quality just isn't there. If you live in the United States, the Natural Wine Company in Brooklyn ships via FedEx Ground and offers a good selection of wines from around the world, many of which are sustainable, biodynamic, and organic.

Perhaps the best thing about French wine is that you really don't need to know that much. You don't need to memorize grape varietals or brand names or who the latest trendy winemaker is. Pick a price point, pick a region, and dive in. If you like that bottle, Google "wine map of France" and start exploring other wines in that region. The names of the towns are the names of the wines, making the whole process simple and quite enjoyable (traveling of the palate, if you will). Unlike California wines, each wine that you pick from a particular area of France will be a distinct representation of that place.

French wine can be approachable and affordable if you look for smaller producers and less well-known wine varietals. As compared to the New World, there are still many wine regions in Europe that remain relatively untouched by *le marketing*. Ideally, a winery will make wine and then price it accordingly, instead of figuring out what price the market will bear and then making wine to fit what the general public's palates and wallets dictate. Great values can be had when you venture into unfamiliar territory in your local wine shop.

Olivier Magny writes in *Into Wine*,

> If wine is music, the soil is the composer and the winemaker is the conductor. For the concert to sound great, it takes the conductor having a very intimate relationship with the part. But it also takes the record company not asking the conductor to make Beethoven sound like Snoop Dogg—simply because "this is what people like these days."[42]

But being from California, I love me some Snoop, and I've learned to appreciate Beethoven along the way. There is a time and a place for both genres. This analogy, I think, is a perfect segue into the world of rosé.

I still giggle a bit when I think of the rosé shortage "crisis" in the Hamptons a couple of summers ago. It's easy to poke fun at, but really we shouldn't, because what summer dinner or party is complete without it? Rosé is summer in a glass.

It is a mood wine, though certainly not a serious mood, because it's meant to be enjoyed only in warm weather. Provence is the main wine region that it is associated with, although there are others, including some great options from Long Island. This is the one instance in which I recommend not thinking too much about it and instead grabbing whatever bottle is convenient. Unless you work in the wine industry or you're a rosé aficionado, you're probably not going to notice the difference. If you are truly tasting it, you're probably not drinking it in the right setting. It's all about fun. It should be enjoyed on the beach, or poolside, on a sun-soaked terrace while relaxing with family, or at a party catching up with friends. What does it pair well with? White jeans and bikinis, obviously.

A white Burgundy is not something you can compare to a rosé because that's like comparing apples to oranges. And white Burgundy is certainly not something you can discuss alongside the chardonnays cranked out by New World conglomerates because that's like comparing apples to an apple-flavored snack pack. White Burgundy, or *Bourgogne blanc*, is chardonnay (while red Burgundy is pinot noir). Burgundy's Côte d'Or is comprised of the Côte de Nuits and the Côte de Beaune, the latter of which is home of the world's most lust-worthy white wines.

This region boasts many varying layers of earth that date back millions and millions of years, like a *millefeuille* of soil and clay that's a tasty treat for the water-starved vines. The growers in the area respect the super soil that they're standing on and use it to coax the best possible grapes out of the land. Irrigation is an absolute no-no in really great wine regions such as Bourgogne because dry soil forces the vines to dig deeper in search of moisture and absorb all of that goodness. The kid who graduates college without a dime in his pocket and with mounds of student loans to pay is going to hit the ground running looking for work, while his friend with the trust fund is more likely to cruise around and party for a while. If given the choice, I'd rather work with the first kid, and I'd pick Bourgogne blanc over California chardonnay any day.

Some white-wine stunners from the region include Meursault, Puligny-Montrachet, Chassagne-Montrachet, and Montrachet. But these are by no means budget wines. The good news is that chardonnay from Burgundy in general is really quite good at all price points. For more affordable versions, stay away from the Côte de Beaune and look toward the Côte Chalonnaise and Mâconnais. You can Google "map of Burgundy," learn some villages in these areas, and start experimenting.

Chablis is technically part of the Burgundy region, but the style is completely different. I would say it's closer in style to a Sancerre, even though it's still chardonnay. It's the northernmost region of Burgundy, and as such, the wine is much more crisp and acidic (cooler climates equal more acidic wines, while as you go south, warmer climates equal ripe, stronger, more fruit-forward wines). Chablis can be a great example of a wine that offers freshness and minerality but without the sometimes supertart, over-the-top acidity that so many white wines today have. A young Chablis will still pack an acid punch that pairs well with shellfish and citrusy dishes, but older ones boast a roundness that is more in line with classic aged white Burgundies.

If you are squeezing lemon juice all over something, such as a light fish dish, Sancerre will be a no-fail match. Made mostly from sauvignon blanc, white Sancerre is fairly straightforward and doesn't have as much variance as Burgundies do. There is obviously a difference between the top-of-the-line *crus* and table-wine versions but not as much as I would expect from a French wine region. I spent three weeks in Sancerre once, and after week one, it all began to taste similar. In a nutshell, if you reach for a Sancerre, you pretty much know what you're getting, so it can be a reliable friend for certain dishes.

Other than Sancerre, France offers many other high-acid white-wine options, such as wines made from chenin blanc in the Loire. If you're looking for something that's fresh and light but interesting, the Loire is an excellent region to explore. It offers a ton of hidden gems at affordable price points. Meanwhile, if you're looking for something that's rounder and slightly funky, white wine from Jura can be just the thing. The cooler climate and relatively under-the-radar status make for some delicious offerings. White wines from the Loire and Jura are pretty dependable matches with spicy food and Asian food.

Another excellent pairing with Asian food or spicy food is a riesling from Alsace. The classic advice with wine and food pairings is to pair opposites or similarities, nothing in between, so pair food that's spicy or acidic with a spicy or acidic wine to match it, or pair it with a sweeter wine to tame it. This is similar to relationships. Don't go with something (or someone) boring just because. Find an equal match or tame the bad boy you want.

Speaking of bad boys, Bordeaux has gained quite the reputation these days because of its splashy auction prices and issues with counterfeiting. The region's first-growth classification of 1855 provides clear markers of status, which is a key factor of its overwhelming popularity in Asia (and anywhere else in the world where people are into that sort of thing). The first-growth, or *premier cru*, ranking is simple to follow because there are only five in total: Château Haut-Brion, Château Lafite Rothschild, Château Latour, Château Margaux, and Mouton Rothschild.

Bordeaux is an outlier among Old World wines in the sense that it has become almost more of a brand than a place. And each of these five first-growth wines are very powerful brands on their own, often acquired just for the labels and bought and displayed by collectors from around the world in order to convey wealth and status. Bordeaux is excellent at marketing, but its difference dates back to that decision in 1855. Whereas other French wines tend to be classified and referred to in terms of *terroir*, the *premier cru* classification was determined by a château's reputation and the price of its wine.

I have met collectors who buy these branded wines clearly just for sport, for the sake of buying and showing but not necessarily truly enjoying. You can easily identify them because they drink the same wines over and over, and when discussing Bordeaux wine, they refer to the names on the bottles (e.g., Château Lynch-Bages or Pétrus) versus the regions (e.g., Pauillac or Pomerol). So the classic wines of Bordeaux have become commodities, which is a shame but an inevitable one given the brand recognition and limited quantities.

Beyond the first-growth wines, Bordeaux has a long history with many different regions and classifications, so it is difficult to sum up, but for simplicity's sake, we can divide it into the left bank and the right bank. Cabernet sauvignon dominates the left bank, while merlot and cabernet franc play supporting roles. The main left-bank red wines are Pauillac, Margaux, Saint-Estèphe, and Saint-Julien. Pessac-Léognan is often considered to be a left-bank red because it's a similar style and is adjacent to this region. This is a lot to keep in mind when wine shopping, but when I was first learning about Bordeaux, I remembered them as Paul, Margot, Stephanie, Julien, and Leo, and that helped. The right bank is dominated by merlot, with a bit of cabernet franc and cabernet sauvignon blended in. Key right-bank Bordeaux wines are Saint-Émilion and Pomerol.

I'm a *rive gauche* girl myself. I often find the merlot-dominant wines of the right bank to be far too heavy on the cherry flavors, and I just don't think they have the balance that left-bank Bordeaux does, but of course there are always exceptions. To me, this sums up the best part about French wines: you can identify which regions you prefer and which you don't, and that serves as a very handy mental guide for ordering and buying wine.

Burgundy is far more nuanced and yet simultaneously more minimalist than Bordeaux. One is brain; the other is brawn. If I want to really savor a glass of wine on its own, it will always be Burgundy, because I've found that good ones offer the ideal combination of balance and intrigue in a way that no other wine can. If it's cold outdoors and I'm serving a rich, slow-cooked meat dish indoors, Bordeaux is ideal. Or a hearty Italian Barolo, but I digress.

The red wines of Bourgogne (the French name for Burgundy) are all pinot noir. As such, if the grape-growing process does not go smoothly one year, it is difficult for winemakers to correct the flaws because they're not blending with other varietals. Red Burgundy is for purists who really want to taste the variations from vineyard to vineyard, year to year. Those who are obsessed with *terroir* are almost always obsessed with Bourgogne *rouge*. The aromas in a glass of Burgundy always entice and yet stump me, and that is my favorite part. You're not hit over the head with one smell or one flavor. Its power lies in its subtlety and its complexity. The main easy-to-find red Burgundy wines are Vosne-Romanée, Gevrey-Chambertin, Nuits-Saint-Georges, Chambolle-Musigny, Pommard, Aloxe-Corton, and Volnay.

If you haven't had much experience with red French wine, red Burgundy is not the ideal place to start (as opposed to white Burgundy, which is pleasing from the first sip). Anticipating and experiencing the delights and disappointments of single-varietal red wines is a thrilling—and sometimes expensive—process of trial and error, so it's not necessarily the best starting place.

If you are used to New World wines, a good place to begin is the southern Rhone. Many people—and I am one of them—seem to start with Châteauneuf-du-Pape as a gateway into French reds. It is an easy transition from a big, juicy, spicy zinfandel from California into a more toned-down and yet still-heady Châteauneuf-du-Pape. It is kind of the zinfandel of the French wine world, except wine has been grown in this region for a very long time. The people, the soil, and the vines know what they're doing, so it's kind of an unfair comparison. Châteauneuf-du-Pape *rouge* is made mostly from a blend of grape varietals, including but not at all limited to grenache noir, mourvèdre, syrah, and cinsault. The blending of so many varietals allows the winemakers to turn out more consistent people-pleasing wines year after year, which is one reason that they make a great gateway.

Red wine from the northern Rhone, meanwhile, is made mostly from syrah. Côte-Rôtie, Cornas, and Hermitage are all excellent red

Rhones that are easy to drink yet still weighty. They are the next logical step after Châteauneuf-du-Pape because they fall somewhat in between that and Bordeaux. They're still fruit forward and powerful but with a lot more finesse. They pair perfectly with meat dishes that have some sort of fruit or sweet component, such as a tagine or a duck dish.

Another thing to look into when tasting and experimenting with different wines is biodynamics. Based on principles created by Austrian philosopher Rudolf Steiner in the 1920s, biodynamics is an approach to wine that takes into account the entire vineyard and all of its flora and fauna. It involves harvesting in line with solar and lunar cycles. Random, I know, but there's something to be said for it, because these wines certainly express their *terroir*, and that is a beautiful thing—in theory and in my mouth. The approach is holistic and a bit hippie, and I love it. That is not to say that biodynamic wine is necessarily better than other wines. If I were debating between two wines and one was biodynamic, I would definitely go with that one, but I wouldn't choose a wine just because it's biodynamic, if that makes sense.

These wines often appear on wine lists and in wine shops around organic, natural, and sustainable wines. "Organic" means the wine was made using organically grown grapes, while natural wine is supposed to be made with minimal intervention and without additives (though sulfites are allowed in some cases). While biodynamics looks at the vineyard as a whole, sustainable winegrowers look at the world as a whole, incorporating practices that are feasible and positive for the environment and humanity in the long term.

There is also an implication that fewer sulfites are used in these types of wines, but that's not always true. Really, the best way to find what suits you is via personal experimentation. For example, my favorite wine shops tend to be the ones that offer biodynamic and sustainable wines, but that doesn't necessarily mean that's what I buy once I'm in the shop. I find a certain comfort in shopping or dining at establishments that at least consider these things and know what they're talking about. Just like buying nonorganic produce from a local farmer is better than buying organic produce from a farming conglomerate (in my opinion), buying wine from a smaller producer that a trusted wine expert recommends is probably going to be more pleasing than buying a certified organic wine that practically every wine shop carries.

If you're new to wine and would like to learn more, I can give you a Wine Tasting 101 lesson in one word: "drink." Unless you're studying to become a sommelier, the only thing you need to do in the beginning is start tasting. I have attended countless "intro to wine" classes, and they usually walk through the same exact steps, drawn out in a way that does not befit the beginner. The instructor will often start with a narrative about color, telling you to hold the glass up in front of a white sheet of paper and observe the shade. But you really don't need to think about color when you're beginning your wine journey. If you don't have a reference point yet on taste, the color won't mean much. As you gain experience, you will begin to pay attention to color naturally, and not because an instructor told you to, but because it will be a great indication as to whether it's the kind of wine you're in the mood for.

You also don't need to be taught how to swirl wine because it's just awkward in the beginning, and that too will come naturally with time and observation. By the same token, yes, smelling before drinking is very important to a wine lover because it provides clues as to what's in the glass and is an enjoyable thing to do before sips and in between sips. But beginners do not really need to be taught this because it will become second nature with practice. Smelling what we're sipping, and enjoying the process, is an instinctual thing once the base level of taste is in place. If you're new to wine, or new to Old

World wine, you can create your own introduction to the subject just by opening a bottle and enjoying it.

A last thought on wine: I was part of a wine group when I lived in Paris, and the leader guided us to start with "what is it not" to identify the varietal and its qualities. Similarly, sommeliers at restaurants often appreciate when diners begin with what they don't like, making it easier for them to quickly narrow down the wine list to something they do (try this; it's really helpful). This all ties in nicely with being a Francophile. Sometimes you have to try on other cultures in order to find out what you are not. Once you've narrowed that down, it's easy to discover what you like and who you are.

Chapter 13

Jacques-in-the-Box

Many books say that the arrondissements of Paris are laid out like a snail, starting from the first and spiraling out to the twentieth. But Paris is not an *escargot*. It is a box. One big box made up of millions and millions of little boxes. The French put people and things and ideas in boxes all day every day, and they superglue the lids of these boxes shut.

I would say that it's a culturally ingrained hobby, but I don't think they actually realize that they're doing it, or at least the extent of it, so I think it's more habit than hobby. The grossly overused marketing term "think outside the box" surely had to come from someone who attempted to do business in France.

Once while living in Paris, a (pre-Uber) car service that I'd requested via an app refused to pick me up because the driver insisted that the person who had requested the car was most definitely a man. He just could not wrap his brain around the possibility that I was in fact Jordan and that I am a woman. He let me in after a lengthy explanation and an ID flash, but then he lectured me for the entire ride, insisting that I should not have a man's name but instead a more appropriate feminine one. Another time, after going to my annual exam at the gynecologist, I received all of my records via mail. The envelope and letter were addressed to Monsieur Jordan Phillips, and the forms and records had been changed from Madame to Monsieur. At a gynecologist's office. Apparently Jordan simply cannot be a female name in France.

So they even managed to put my box in a box.

I could take the time to explain to every single person that, *oui, je suis une femme, depuis toujours,* and that my name is like "Dominique" in France, which is mostly a *masculin* name but sometimes it can be *féminin.* But that is exhausting to repeat every day to every Guillaume and Marie. Insert shrug. *C'est la vie.*

Lines are constantly drawn in the proverbial sandbox. This is this way; that is that way; this is mine; that is yours. Know your place; pay your dues; don't try to get ahead; don't stand out.

I have a theory that expats who last in Paris secretly like being stereotyped and proving the Parisians wrong, whether it be via mastery of the language or excellence in a non-money-making, Parisian-approved field. But just when you think you've proven yourself and managed to blow the lid open, surprise! There's another one waiting. In order to understand you, the Frenchman must be able to tuck you away and place you neatly on his shelf of compartmentalized mental boxes.

If an expat can look past all of this, Paris provides an excellent quality of life and sense of community. If you take out the bureaucracy and boxes, you are left with a charming city that's full of comforting rituals and cultural excitement. A café can be like a best friend: entertaining you when you're up, consoling you when you're down, people-watching with you when the weather is nice, warming you up when it's cold. The croissants will always be tasty, and crossing the Seine will always be pleasing. Once you find your people, they will stick with you. And whether you're interested in art, design, dance, music, literature, architecture, food, wine, fashion, film, history, or all of the above, there will be more interesting exhibitions and events than you can possibly manage. Paris spoils you with freedom, beauty, and choice.

I was in Paris the week of that horrific series of events on Friday, November 13, 2015, when terrorists gunned down innocent people in an unprecedented attack against all that is good and right in the world. It was the first time I ever felt scared in Paris. My heart was so heavy, and tears kept springing to my eyes when I thought of the victims and their families, of those who survived but had to witness the carnage, and of the Parisians who would have to live alongside the constant reminders in the aftermath. But I saw a comment on an article on the *New York Times* website that somehow made the situation feel ever so slightly better:

France embodies everything religious zealots everywhere hate: enjoyment of life here on earth in a myriad little ways: a fragrant cup of coffee and buttery croissant in the morning, beautiful women in short dresses smiling freely on the street, the smell of warm bread, a bottle of wine shared with friends, a dab of perfume, children paying in the Luxembourg Gardens, the right not to believe in any god, not to worry about calories, to flirt and smoke and enjoy sex outside of marriage, to take vacations, to read any book you want, to go to school for free, to play, to laugh, to argue, to make fun of prelates and politicians alike, to leave worrying about the afterlife to the dead. No country does life on earth better than the French.[43]

If that isn't reason enough to love France, I don't know what is. Those very freedoms that we love and cherish are the same freedoms that some groups find threatening.

Parisians threw open the doors to their homes via #portesouvertes on Twitter, ushering locals and tourists alike into safety. The outpouring of support and camaraderie was a beautiful thing to witness in the face of such tragedy. Those barbarians tried to blow up freedom's blanket of safety, but instead they uncovered a culture of compassion.

This, I believe, is because French people do not necessarily like boxes. They love nothing more than to debate about every single minute detail of every aspect of life. The Frenchman does not just put you in a box on his shelf; he takes that box out and carefully examines it on a regular basis. The underlying reason is not ignorance but conformity. The lid may be superglued shut, but that will not prevent him from inspecting the box to figure out what's really inside. Curiosity breeds compassion.

Ironically, the French penchant for conformity leads to a desire to seek out the unconventional as well. The French are nothing if not full of paradoxes. This is summed up fantastically in the book *How the French Think: An Affectionate Portrait of an Intellectual People.*

These conceptual juggling acts have produced delicious oxymorons and nourished yet another cherished feature of Gallic thinking: the love of paradox. Thanks to this trait, France has given us passionate rationalists, conservative revolutionaries (and revolutionary traditions), violent moderates, secular missionaries, spiritual materialists, *spectateurs engagés* (committed observers), patriotic internationalists, conflictual allies, and collective-minded individualists—and, by virtue of the sometimes unfortunate fate of French armies on the battlefield, from Vercingétorix to the Battle of Waterloo, perhaps the most exquisite paradox of all: the glorious defeat.[44]

As a Gemini, I can appreciate this duality. Why be one thing when you can be two? But taken to extremes, it can be exhausting. So instead of too many boxes and paradoxes, here's to hoping for more slithering snails tucked inside open shells, because nobody likes a square.

There are still many issues with racism in France, especially when it comes to the acceptance of people who don't fit the traditional definition of a French citizen, but I think things are slowly changing, just as they are everywhere in the world. Utopian aspirations abound in France, but often the reality lags far behind, especially with older generations. Maybe one day, no one will care if Dominique is a man or woman, atheist or Muslim, but will see only a human being instead.

Chapter 14

Non

et's pretend we're strolling in Paris right now, doing a little window shopping. We've just had an *apéritif* (okay, two), and we're feeling good. Something catches your eye, so we pop into a little boutique that looks *hyper sympa*. We're greeted by a handsome guy wearing skinny jeans, a skinny shirt, and a skinny tie. Serge Gainsbourg and Jane Birkin's *"Je t'aime...moi non plus"* listlessly trickles down from overhead. You get caught up in the moment and buy some supercool boots even though they are quite a splurge. You're sure they will make you look like a Parisienne. They don't have your size, but the skinny-tie guy convinces you that the leather will stretch out once you break them in.

The next day, sans drinks and sans Serge, you try on the boots again, and it becomes clear that they don't fit you at all. They're actually very uncomfortable. You know you'll never wear these boots, so you grab your receipt and set off to return them. But it's Sunday, so the store is closed. On Monday, you try again, but the store is closed for lunch. On Tuesday, you try again, but the skinny-tie guy gives you a resounding *non*.

You bought something in France, and you want to return it? Ha! *C'est pas possible.*

Why on earth would you think you have that right? In France, the customer is not king. The customer is always wrong. This mindset permeates all aspects of life in France, whether it's shopping or trying to accomplish anything, really.

non!   If you are a student in France, you will be continually told that perfection does not exist. The system is built upon criticism. You are not perfect. No one is perfect. You are wrong. Grading works on a subjectively awarded points system out of twenty, with twenty being the best. But nobody gets twenty. In fact, sixteen out of twenty is considered absolutely fantastic. You have to be really smart to consistently score sixteen out of twenty. Believe it or not, twelve out of twenty is not bad. As a point of reference, that would be like scoring 60 percent on a test in the American system. You wouldn't be happy about it, and they aren't either; they're just used to it. Mediocrity is fine because there's no point in trying for perfection. It doesn't exist, remember?

But, technically speaking, you would get a far better education in France. If I had gone to primary school there, I probably wouldn't have had to pull out my phone just now to calculate the percentage for twelve out of twenty. School in France is high pressure, but they learn so much more, and education is gloriously standardized in a way that is unfathomable in the States. We could learn a lot from their system. But it has one fault that completely overshadows its thoroughness: students are not trained to believe that they can take on the world and be anything they want to be. You want to be *what* when you grow up? No. That's not realistic.

An entire upbringing of learning that you can't get twenty out of twenty no matter how hard you try takes its toll. The effects ripple into adulthood and seep into all aspects of French life. Whereas New Yorkers show their power by saying yes, connecting people, and making things happen, Parisians show their power by saying no.

I like the word "yes," and I constantly use the word "perfect." Does dinner on Tuesday at 8:00 p.m. sound good? Sounds perfect! How do these boots look on me? Perfect.

So why did I fall in love with a country whose culture is so, well, belittling? I suppose I like a challenge. All of the good ones take work.

The first time I ran away from home, I was two years old. I don't remember it, obviously, but my mother has told me the story many times. Apparently I was fed up with being told no, so I announced that I was leaving for good. My mother calmly said that if that's what I really wanted, she'd help me pack. She pulled out her favorite suitcase and pointed out all of the things I would need for wherever I was going. But I didn't know where I was going. And after she told me good-bye and good luck, I tried with all of my might to push the heavy suitcase off our front porch and onto the sidewalk, but that's as far as I got.

I don't know where it comes from, but my instinct has always been to run away. Why face a problem when you can just pretend that it doesn't exist?

Sometimes the running away can be figurative, as in shutting someone out. Other times the running away is literal. Feeling lost at home sucks; feeling lost somewhere else is exciting. Perhaps there's a common thread among people who are addicted to travel or who desire to live in another country: you don't have to deal with everything if you don't stick around.

Paris is a great place for wandering around aimlessly when you're feeling down or confused. Whether you're observing the gray sky as it meets up with the gray buildings and the gray sidewalks or hearing Édith Piaf's earthy voice bellowing out lyrics of loss and love, you can feel right at home while moping about in Paris. Unlike in the United States, you're not expected to smile all the time or put on a good face. It is completely acceptable to whine, even to total strangers. Nearly one-third of the French population takes antianxiety pills or similar medications, either regularly or on occasion.[45] France is a country of *râleurs* (complainers), and Parisians are the champions. I don't know if they were always this way or if it's more of a postwar thing due to the marked decline in French power and glory ever since then. Regardless, it is a city that welcomes melancholy with open arms.

Is this a bad quality or a good one? I can't decide. Sometimes grace and tenderness can be found in sadness. As Anna Karina's character Angéla exclaims in Jean-Luc Godard's *Une femme est une femme*, nothing is more beautiful than a woman in tears.

So don't be afraid that Paris will find out what you're really like. Because Paris does not judge you. Its inhabitants sure will, but the city itself will never patronize you for feeling sad. And when you're ready to feel good again, Paris will always be there for you, offering beauty to behold and growth to be had.

Living there as an expat cracks you open like one of those empty coconut shells found during walks on the beach. As you fall from your comfortable perch, your insides become exposed and vulnerable, and you are forced to change. There's no going back to eating ranch dressing again. Your taste in everything changes, from food to art to friends to clothing. Your view of the world changes, and so does the way the world views you.

My favorite part of the movie *Sabrina*—the 1954 version—is when Sabrina (played by Audrey Hepburn) is writing a letter to her father at the end of her two years studying in Paris, calling them the most wonderful years of her life. Before living in Paris, this part inspired me; after having lived in Paris for two years, this part makes my eyes well up with tears every time.

I shall always love you for sending me here. It is late at night and someone across the way is playing "*La Vie en Rose.*" It is the French way of saying, "I'm looking at the world through rose-colored glasses," and it says everything I feel. I have learned so many things, Father, not just how to make vichyssoise or calf's head with sauce vinaigrette, but a much more important recipe: I have learned how to live, how to be in the world and of the world, and not just to stand aside and watch. And I will never, never again run away from life, or from love either.

Chapter 15

Le Bon Goût

The real French paradox has nothing to do with red wine or butter, but it does have to do with taste. In the United States, people often consider things to be in good taste when they are in the presence of money. Expensive equals good. Good taste in Paris has nothing to do with money; it is the absence of vulgarity. And this is not just a Coco Chanel mantra but an inherently Parisian way of viewing people, places, and things.

The paradox is that they do appreciate the finer things in life but only if no one is actually enjoying those fine things. Upon seeing a luxurious article of clothing or an expensive decorative *objet*, a Parisian can acknowledge the craftsmanship, artistry, and tradition that went into creating it. But someone actually buying and using that beautiful thing? That's in bad taste. Money is bad. People with money are really bad.

Imagine a Bordeaux-fueled, foie-gras-filled, over-the-top Michelin-starred meal created by one of Paris's many great culinary masters. Show a picture of that meal to Parisians, and they will think that it looks delicious, commenting on the excellent presentation. A masterpiece! What a fine gastronomic feat. Show the same picture to Americans, and they'll think, wow, that looks fancy. Yum! Now show an image of the same meal to the Americans but with a person included—the person who is eating that meal. Still, yum! That looks tasty. Can we jump into that picture? Show the same image to Parisians, and boy does the sentiment change. What an a———hole! Who has that kind of money to spend on a meal? How gluttonous.

Perhaps a more concrete example is a Parisien's relationship with cars. Many French men seem to be kind of into cars, which is surprising given that no self-respecting Parisian would drive around town in an expensive sports car, not even a billionaire. Especially not a billionaire. If a Parisien sees a flashy car, he will naturally be curious and want to check it out. He might nod in approval of its exterior curves and impressive interior. But then he realizes that some rich *con* actually owns that car. So of course he keys it.

In New York—the concrete jungle where dreams are made—you can eat anything, drive anything, wear anything, or say anything. No one will blink. In the past, the development of what was considered good taste was a gradual process that took several generations. But now that process has been sped up, and people can more or less buy or talk their way into (or out of) whatever they desire. You don't even have to be rich to get what you want; you can just be crafty. To borrow from the great marketer Jean-Noël Kapferer, "Luxury is about knowing how to spend, rather than having spending power."[46]

Americans consider the whole rags-to-riches bit to be very positive. We love these types of stories as long as they're more *Shark Tank* than *American Greed*. Though not everyone has the same opportunity, most everyone in America can be relatively successful with a little luck and a lot of hard work, and we love seeing that theory proven true.

Meanwhile, Paris is the city of suppressed dreams. The city of *non*. Those who didn't attend a *grande école* don't really stand a chance to "make it big" because they didn't get into one, and those who did attend one don't really stand a chance because those places breed conformity (and bureaucrats). What was once a city of glorious intellectual defiance has become one of routine defiance. Standing up for your principles is one thing; saying no just for the sake of saying no is another.

But it wasn't always this way.

Though being born into an aristocratic family was the only way to enjoy the finer things in life during many points of France's history, seventeenth-century Paris was a playground for self-made men. Suddenly social reinvention became possible through money. The finest homes were filled with nouveaux riches, businessmen who worked their way up (though sometimes via questionable means).

"Fake it 'til you make it" was the name of the game at first, with the emphasis on buying things to look the part and blend in with the blue bloods. But then the carriages, clothing, and mansions of these newly minted princes of finance and barons of real estate started becoming more opulent than those of the most prominent aristocrats. It was a relatively quick reshuffling of the previously impenetrable social class system, and suddenly Paris was teeming with parvenus. But they didn't buy just mansions; they also bought titles. Many financiers purchased their nobility, thus blurring the rungs on the social ladder even further. It didn't go over very well in some circles.

In the eighteenth century, the aristocratic (and faux-risto-cratic) lifestyle was questioned, big-time. There was the Age of Enlightenment (1715–1789) and the *sans-culottes* and the French

Revolution. It was a time for reflection and survival, certainly not a time for material aspiration.

Fast-forward to the mid-nineteenth century, and social mobility was back in fashion. Paris was full of residents from all walks of life. According to Stephane Kirkland of *Paris Reborn: Napoléon III, Baron Haussmann, and the Quest to Build a Modern City*,

> High society was animated by a full contingent of dukes and duchesses, marquis and marquises, counts and countesses, and so on. But the bourgeoisie so well described by Balzac was also emerging, from the rich bankers and factory owners to the upwardly mobile provincials. There were the military men, the clergy, the journalists, the artists, the actors, the students, the women of moderate virtue, and a growing class of workers. Lifestyles ran the gamut, from the stultified salons of the aristocracy to the wild taverns of the Latin Quarter to the popular dance halls outside the city gates in Belleville. Never has Paris had quite the same vitality, the same sense of a society in flux, where anything was possible.[47]

It sounds a bit like New York today.

La Belle Époque (1871–1914) occurred during a period of optimism, peace, and political stability. The era saw numerous advances in science and technology. Successful businessmen continued to become nouveaux riches, and as in the seventeenth century, they observed and emulated the elite social class. Culture flourished, as did the lifestyles of the bourgeoisie.

Outside of the bourgeoisie and the upper class, there was still much entertainment to be had. Bistros and music halls were popular, as were Paris's still-famous cabarets. This was the heyday of the Moulin Rouge, where—in a stark contrast to other cities around the world—burlesque performances were considered more normal than risqué.

The Art Nouveau movement, typified by not-quite-lucid swirled lines and a penchant for nature, captures the spirit of this era at all levels of society. If you look at the art, furniture, or architecture from that period, you'll notice that it isn't all rigid and symmetrical. It's daring and fun and full of movement.

Prior to my first trip to Paris, I saw Baz Luhrmann's *Moulin Rouge*, causing me to dream of the Belle Époque and absinthe-fueled writers pulling all-nighters. I wanted to jump into one of those Toulouse-Lautrec posters filled with vibrant cancan girls dancing and people kissing. Never mind that the kisses were often paid for and the writers were often depressed. It was Bohemian. This is perhaps why I still sometimes view the city nostalgically and romantically, through sepia-toned glasses. Paris might not offer a good paycheck, but it always offers the possibility for adventure.

Far from the unconventional enclave of Montmartre, the city's rich and wannabe rich gathered at Maxim's Paris, where Champagne was the drink of choice. It was a place to see and be seen. The fashion was over the top and glamorous. Not far from Maxim's, the term "ritzy" was invented at the Ritz Paris in the Place Vendôme, where an exclusive clientele gathered to show off their latest purchases and enjoy Auguste Escoffier's modern *haute cuisine*.

This ritzy Paris—the one of Maxim's and Champagne and Birkin bags and macarons—is the one in the minds of the millions of tourists who flock to the French capital to get a taste of the good life. But that is not the Paris of Parisians. Today, taste is dictated by strict social codes. Subtle equals good. Many wealthy Parisians drive around in beat-up cars and eschew flashy clothing and jewelry. Think of the excess and ostentation in America in the 1980s versus the minimalism and discretion of the 1990s, but the difference is far more extreme. Yes, the economy has a lot to do with it, but in France, the history runs much deeper. Their progression toward sobriety is on a much longer, grander scale.

One of the biggest lessons that Paris has to offer is the art of camouflage. Step one: learn how to blend in. Step two: decide whether you want to or not. Going right to step two can lead to making some unfortunate fashion mistakes. Going through step one and choosing whether or not to reject social norms is different from skipping step one altogether. Whether we're talking fashion or philosophy, manners or morals, it's helpful to know the rules first in order to break them successfully.

So whether you spend time in Paris learning the myriad unspoken societal norms or you carefully study them from afar, the city and its history have a lot to offer. You'll acquire knowledge and the ability to decide what is right for you. You'll acquire power. After step two, if you decide to be a rebel, you will be one with a cause.

Chapter 16

La Mode, La Mode, La Mode

B uying clothing will not make you instantly part of a community, nor will it make you happy per se, but spending money on an exquisitely well-made item that you will be proud to wear year after year can bring a certain amount of pleasure. Spending just to spend is frivolous, but buying a few quality basics or must-have items can make you look and feel great.

Prior to the 1970s, each society generally grasped on to one fashion trend at a time. The introduction of different trends came not just because of polarized political views but also from the true beginning of mass production in clothing, often with inexpensive fabrics, such as polyester. Each subculture in society adopted its own style of dress, which we now consider to be a normal mode of self-expression. A punk's rebellious clothing, hairstyle, and piercings might seem daring until you consider that he is dressed just like everyone else in his group. He is, in effect, a sheep following the crowd, albeit a less mainstream one.

According to the *Stanford Law Review*, "The desire to be 'in fashion'—most visibly manifested in the practice of dress—captures a significant aspect of social life, characterized by both the pull of continuity with others and the push of innovation toward the new."[48]

Fashion is a way to convey who you are. What you wear displays what socioeconomic class you belong to or what socioeconomic class you *want* to belong to. Wearing or using certain items calls out to others who are similar, whether overtly or discreetly.

A friend taught me about the concept of *ça vaut le coup*, which I then heard frequently around Paris. Referring to "value for money," *ça vaut le coup* can be used in the context of an expensive item that can be "worth it" if it is very special. Even if a Parisienne is on a tight budget, she is willing to spend extra for an exquisite dinner or a well-fitting leather motorcycle jacket (called a *perfecto*) as long as she finds value.

This type of jacket is the cornerstone of one of the two main off-duty Parisienne looks: rock chic, which almost always involves jeans and a *perfecto*, and *bobo* (short for *bourgeoise bohème*), which is basically Bohemian hipster. The BCBG (*bon chic bon genre*) style—that is, classic—is now mostly seen on Parisiennes over the age of fifty, though it can still be spotted on younger women in the sixteenth arrondissement or as appropriate office attire throughout Paris.

France most definitely does not have an #OOTD culture. Wearing basically the same thing every day is not considered odd; the uniform approach comes across as possession of a good sense of style and self-knowledge. This way of dressing is very practical because it's really easy to look chic with a few key pieces, often called a capsule wardrobe. Then as your budget and desire increases, you can add in more high-quality, well-made basics, always making sure that they're pieces that work with what you already have and that you can (and will) wear over and over. And make sure that you really love every single one. All white T-shirts are not the same, so never settle. Wait until you find the absolutely perfect white T-shirt that's comfortable and flattering, buy two, and wear them all the time.

I once observed a Frenchwoman wearing the exact same white jeans and flats nearly every single day for an entire summer. She looked good, and she obviously couldn't care less that she was a serial outfit repeater. So why should we? I officially give you permission to wear things that you love constantly with reckless abandon. Just think how much easier your morning routine will be.

Buy clothing and accessories that last, and don't be shy about repeating looks. This will change your relationship with yourself, others around you, and the environment. Trendy fast fashion purchased on impulse is often far less personal than a high-quality, timeless item that you longed for before buying.

By focusing on quality and fit instead of fashion trends, you can avoid the feeling of constantly needing new clothing. Consumers tend to flock to buy new clothes because their existing clothes seem outdated, not because they need them.[49] Choosing more timeless pieces that fit in with your personal style and collecting them slowly over time will help you build your ideal faux French wardrobe.

The American way of acquiring and wearing clothes is completely different from the French way. It's bad in the sense that it can be unhealthy (for both bank accounts and the environment) and ineffective because having too many options can lead to lengthy or poor decision-making processes. But the American way is good in the sense that dressing up and experimenting with personal style is one of the perks of being a woman, and everyone in Paris kind of looks the same. Frankly, the Parisian way is quite boring. Because freedom of expression is important, your clothing should reflect your personality and current stage of life. And it should be fun!

I think the best approach is to get your basic capsule wardrobe squared away, and then add in some fabulous and funky American-style pieces as your budget allows. But first, start with a full closet cleanout. Go over everything with a critical eye, keeping your new goals in mind, and be merciless.

Before tossing aside something you're not in love with, know that outdated looks from your own closet can have quite a bit of potential. If a garment is well made but out of style, think of simple alterations that can make it current. If a certain denim style is passé, have your tailor change the length to create a "new" pair. Skirt lengths are ever changing; taking a few inches off a skirt or having your tailor slightly alter the proportion can create an updated look that you might love, at a fraction of the price and environmental cost of buying new. Similarly, lopping the sleeves off a blouse or changing a collar can make a tired work outfit into something fresh for the weekends and breathe new life into a neglected garment.

According to Ray A. Smith of the *Wall Street Journal*, people generally wear only about 20 percent of the clothes in their closets on a regular basis. He also notes that research has found that the conventional wisdom that shoppers regret splurges isn't true. Instead, over the long term, shoppers most regretted passing up an indulgence for something practical or less expensive.[50] This contributes to the feeling of having a closet full of mediocrity.

Before making any more fashion purchases, stop to think about your lifestyle, values, and goals. Who are your style icons? What is your look? How do you want people to describe your style? Do you love your current style, or would you like to evolve your look so that your exterior is more reflective of your interior? Who do you want to be this year, next year, in ten years? Now is the time to think about your style in a broader sense and start dressing for the life you want. What is your body type, and what parts do you want to highlight? You are more likely to keep something in your closet for a long time if it helps you look your best. You can prioritize what is important to you, shop according to what you are most passionate about, and then create a wardrobe that helps you become the person you want to be.

Feeling good in your clothing can boost confidence and positive feelings about your body. In a perfect world, we shouldn't need clothes to make us feel good, but they just do. Clothing is functional in that it protects us (e.g., a warm coat in winter), but it accomplishes so much more than that. The right clothing covers our insecurities and emphasizes our assets. Everyone's body is different and beautiful in its own way, and all types should be cherished and appreciated. Well-chosen clothing is one of the most fun ways to celebrate our bodies. When you put on a favorite little black dress that you feel comfortable and sexy in, doesn't it change the way you carry yourself that night?

One day I realized that I had quite a few items of clothing that didn't suit my body type, things I had bought more to be in style than to be true to what looks good on my figure. I went through my closet and challenged every single piece: did I buy this just because (or because of a sale or because a salesperson talked me into something or to follow a trend), or did I buy it because it looked great on me? I cleared out everything that didn't make the cut and consigned it with The RealReal and my local Second Time Around. If an item doesn't make you feel fantastic when you put it on, do yourself a favor and get rid of it.

When creating, or paring down to, the perfect capsule wardrobe, know that it's totally okay to combine black, brown, navy, and gray. For some reason, Americans often get stuck on the idea that certain colors go with black and certain colors go with brown, but it actually looks cool to mix these colors instead of always matching them. For example, all-black clothing paired with low-heeled brown boots and a gray scarf is timeless and fashionable and very Parisian.

Once you have your closet of basics set up, you can infuse a little fun. Twice per year, just as either warmer weather or colder weather is approaching, check out the runway shows online, on Pinterest, or in a favorite fashion magazine, and pick one (or a few, depending on your budget) trend piece and wear it like crazy for the whole season.

Here are some basics to help you create your Parisian capsule wardrobe:

Little White T-Shirt

Images of Jane Birkin wearing shrunken white T-shirts make regular appearances in my Pinterest feed. Sometimes the shirt is tucked into faded, flared-leg jeans, and sometimes it's knotted in front to create a crop top. Sometimes the sleeves are rolled up, sometimes not. (This being Jane Birkin, the one constant is the lack of a bra.)

She mastered the art of finding basic shirts that suited her figure and wearing them numerous different ways. Even more impressively, she made simple things look sexy. Find the perfect white T-shirt, make sure it still looks great after you wash it, and if so, buy an extra in white and two in black. These T-shirts can really become the base for your whole wardrobe because you can dress them up with a blazer or dress them down with denim. They'll serve as undershirts to keep you warm in winter and as starring pieces to keep you cool in summer. If one of them gets to the point where you think it looks too tired (or stained or full of moth holes), make it your go-to workout or around-the-house shirt and buy a fresh one.

White Cotton Button-Down Shirt

Another Jane Birkin staple is the classic white button-down. Your style, budget, and day-to-day life will determine whether it is an oversized shirt "borrowed" from a man's closet or a perfectly tailored work-appropriate one with gleaming white mother-of-pearl buttons.

The great thing about a white button-down shirt is its versatility. At work, you can wear the sleeves in the full-length proper way, the shirt tucked in, and all but the top button buttoned. Headed to happy hour? Roll up the sleeves and unbutton a button or two. Recycle the shirt by pairing it with jeans over the weekend, wearing it tied in a knot at your waist. Pop the collar if you're feeling sassy.

Black Silk Button-Down Blouse

This is a good piece to have when you don't know what to wear. Worn with a blazer, it gives you instant polish when headed to a big meeting or a formal event. Worn with jeans, it becomes the ultimate appropriate-yet-sexy go-to item that will suit a variety of occasions, whether it's heading to a friend's home for dinner or going on a date.

If a silk blouse feels too formal for you, another option is a semi-sheer black blouse that ties at the neck. You can wear it with a camisole underneath for an elegant evening look or with just a black bra and jeans for a casual evening look.

Denim Button-Down Shirt

Both trendy and timeless, the blue denim button-down shirt has become a uniform staple for many a stylish woman (and man). There are countless ways to wear a denim shirt, especially now that denim-on-denim has shed its "Canadian tuxedo" reputation. Once this look has passed its moment, you can still wear your denim shirt as a summer cover-up or light jacket for decades to come.

Think of a new denim shirt as a hit song. It makes you happy every time you hear it, perhaps you play it on repeat for months, and then it becomes well worn and you get tired of it. But years later, you will be happy when you start playing it again, and it will bring you good memories through the decades. Like the songs we love, we associate memories with clothes. Bringing out something you wore on your first date has the same effect as playing the song you first kissed to. Instead of buying trendy fast fashion items, buy pieces that make you happy. Make great memories in them, and then store them away for a bit. The memories will always be there, whether in one year or ten.

Striped Shirt

Just like white jeans, nautical Breton-inspired stripes are trendy practically every summer. You can be sure that if you buy a great little blue-and-white-striped top, you will pull it out year after year to wear beginning in spring.

The classic striped shirt was originally part of the uniform for French navy men in Brittany, and the original design (called *marin-ière*) had twenty or twenty-one stripes. It then became popular with seamen across the region of Northern France for its ease of wear and visibility. After a visit to the French coast, Coco Chanel introduced the garment to the yachting world in 1917,[51] and the striped shirt became an option for both men and women of the haute bourgeoisie. In the 1930s, the shirt became popular with European and American socialites vacationing on the French Riviera, who used it as a chic take on sailor style. It turned "city" decades later through the beatnik scene on the *rive gauche* and it became synonymous with Parisian style. Luminaries like Jean-Paul Sartre, Edie Sedgwick, Andy Warhol, and Audrey Hepburn helped make the striped shirt an international sensation.[52]

Have you seen Jean Seberg in *À Bout de Souffle* (a.k.a. *Breathless*)? The stripes in this film are just so good. Oh, and if you happen to come across a good vintage *New York Herald Tribune* sweater, buy it for me, and I'll pay you double.

Cashmere Sweater

Before making your next purchase, think about what you want out of the garment. What type of climate do you live in, and what is your lifestyle? What do you want your clothing to do for you? If you are buying a sweater that is meant to keep you warm and it's a thin acrylic blend, it won't accomplish what you need it to and probably won't last very long. Meanwhile, a wool or cashmere sweater might be more of an investment, but it will keep you warmer, last a lot longer, and look better.

When I moved from Southern California to a cooler climate, I learned very quickly that cotton just doesn't cut it in the cold. My previous method to keep warm was to just pile on layer after layer, but I learned that wearing cashmere and wool (not mixed with acrylics or mysterious blends) was the way to stay warm in winter. I later learned by trial and error that cashmere and wool keep me warm in the cold and linen keeps me cool in the heat.

Cashmere comes from the combed-out underhair of Kashmir goats. Its use as a textile dates back to the third century BC. It has a lighter weight than other wools, and it provides excellent insulation from the elements. Cashmere is durable, and well-made cashmere garments can last decades. It also resists wrinkling.

A sweater option that is usually more affordable than cashmere is merino wool. Merino is a breed of sheep that has very fine and soft wool. It regulates body temperature, so it is often used in performance wear. It provides warmth without overheating the wearer and also slightly repels moisture. Unlike cotton, it retains its warmth when wet.

Find a comfortable cashmere sweater in a flattering fit, and you will wear it all fall and winter long, year after year. Worn with a T-shirt, it's warm and practical, and worn with only a lacy bra underneath, it's sexy. If you're buying one, go with black, navy, or gray.

Black Cigarette-Fit Jeans or Trousers

Slim and slightly cropped black pants look fantastic with flats and heels alike, making them a must for every wardrobe. They're polished yet casual; they're comfortable yet flattering. Make sure they hit on the right spot at the ankle and that they're not tight at the ankle. Think 1950s bombshell or Audrey Hepburn in *Funny Face*.

Depending on your lifestyle, you can buy them in trouser form (e.g., wool or brushed chino-style cotton) or in a stretchy version (making sure that they aren't so tight that they look like leggings), but I think the denim version is best because you don't have to worry about dry cleaning. Cigarette-fit jeans are very similar to skinny jeans, but the cut is slightly looser and more chic. If your budget allows, buy the same fit in black leather.

White Jeans

White jeans in France are an incredibly common sighting, worn by teenage girls and fiftysomething women alike. It is hands down *the* summer staple. During summer months, white jeans are appropriate in pretty much any situation in any type of weather, barring rainy days because they'll get splattered with mud. They can be dressed up for dinner with heels and a cute top or dressed down with flat sandals and a T-shirt or denim shirt for a day at the park. Make sure your pair isn't too tight; a pair of stretchy, tight white jeans is just tacky. A straight-leg, slightly cropped, slightly relaxed fit is flattering and timeless. When searching for a pair to buy, wear flats to try them on, and make sure they still look good when rolled up.

Denim is made of sturdy cotton twill, a natural woven textile. In addition to its obvious appeal, denim has added benefits for the summer months: it quickly absorbs moisture, it quickly dries, and it has a cooling effect when it's warm.

Relaxed Fit/Boyfriend Jeans

Slouchy boyfriend jeans look good with heels and a cashmere sweater for a casual-but-cool look, and they're nice to have on hand for when you don't feel like putting on something fitted. They're great replacements for sweatpants, making the ideal companion

146

for lounging around at home, going for a walk in the park, or running a quick errand. Parisiennes never go around town in workout clothes or sweatpants, but that doesn't mean that they always dress formally or sacrifice comfort. This is a habit that I've more or less stuck with even after moving back to the United States. It only takes a few seconds to change out of workout clothes, and running errands in jeans, a T-shirt, and flats is just as comfortable as doing so in spandex workout clothes, if not more.

Flared-Leg Jeans

Sometimes it's helpful to look back before moving forward. In fashion, what goes around comes around, and if you're observant and patient, you can build a wardrobe that is on-trend without constantly having to buy new things and chase the trends. If styled in a modern way, thoughtfully selected pieces from your own wardrobe can be wearable decade after decade.

Flared-leg jeans certainly fit into this category. When the clothing of sixties hippies in San Francisco's Haight-Ashbury and New York's Greenwich Village went mainstream and became stylish, it lost its original significance as a form of protest. The youthful bohemian look became an international fashion sensation that shaped the seventies and became embraced by even the most conservative men and women.[53] The widespread popularity of denim—especially the flared-leg kind—is the most prominent aspect of the decade, and obviously denim remains just as pervasive today. Jeans styles change, but like all things fashion, trends are cyclical and almost always return, so when flared-leg jeans go out of style, store them away for the next time around.

Black Flared-Leg Trousers

If you work in a formal environment, investing in a pair of well-fitting black trousers is a necessity. You can wear these week after week all year around with blazers, blouses, and cashmere sweaters.

If you don't work in an office, black flared-leg trousers are still a great option for wearing out to dinner or events, dressed down with a T-shirt or dressed up with a silk button-down blouse.

Denim Shorts

Shorts can be tricky for many women, especially as we get older, but I'm convinced that there's a pair out there for everyone. It can just take time to find. Experiment with different lengths and cuts until you discover just the right pair that you can throw on all summer long, for wearing to the beach or while just lounging around your home. Pair with a denim shirt and wedges for a casual dinner out or with a T-shirt for a casual dinner in.

Black Miniskirt

The originator of the miniskirt was Mary Quant, a London designer whose mod looks became a signature of the swinging sixties. Though the miniskirt is English in origin, no Parisienne-inspired closet is complete without one. How "mini" you go is up to you and your lifestyle. Paired with tights, short skirts are flattering on most everyone. Just make sure to find the right balance of proportions and avoid wearing a miniskirt with sky-high heels and bare legs for daytime. Miniskirts work well with flat boots for daytime or heels for nighttime.

Black Pencil Skirt

Supersexy when paired with a cashmere sweater or a T-shirt and stilettos, the black pencil skirt is an excellent wardrobe staple. To learn how to wear a pencil skirt *à la parisienne*, take notes from Sophie Marceau in the film *Une Rencontre* (Quantum Love). Pencil skirts look good on both slim and curvy bodies, on women of all ages and heights, and they are appropriate for both work (if not too tight) and play. Make sure to avoid wearing your pencil skirt with flat shoes or thick tights, though, because it will look sad and matronly instead of sexy.

LBD

What article of clothing is more versatile than a little black dress? I really can't think of one. Every closet needs one LBD, if not more, budget allowing. It's helpful to have one that's on the sexier side for dates or nights out, one for more conservative evening events, and a versatile one for daytime that looks good with either flats or heels.

Credited to Coco Chanel, the little black dress was made iconic in 1926 when American *Vogue* compared it to a Model T Ford car. It gained further appeal thanks to *Breakfast at Tiffany's*, and the classic style has seen countless variations since.

Black is slimming and easy to keep clean, and it goes with pretty much everything. You can wear all-black accessories, or you can pile on the color. It's simultaneously a sober color and a sexy one, which is what makes it so versatile. Little black dresses don't necessarily need to be little per se; they can be skimpy or they can be multilayered and avant-garde. Really, they're whatever your body type and lifestyle deem appropriate. Perhaps the best thing about an LBD is that once you find one that suits you, it can be a go-to piece in your wardrobe decade after decade.

Denim Jacket

Though totally American, the denim jacket is another staple of the Parisienne's wardrobe. I can't imagine dressing for summer evenings without one; jean jackets just work with everything. If you have the time and interest, finding a vintage one can be a much cheaper (and more original) way to add this piece if you don't have one that you like already.

Blazer

Black and navy-blue blazers are ubiquitous in France. Women of all ages and all sizes wear blazers for daytime and nighttime, all year around. Yes, women in other countries wear them too, but the big difference in France is that practically every woman wears them with T-shirts underneath, and they aren't just worn in professional settings. In the United States, women typically wear blazers when headed to the office, with blouses or lightweight shells or sweaters underneath.

Even if you're wearing a T-shirt and jeans, a blazer will provide instant polish. Women with longer legs always look great in blazers, but women with shorter legs need to be a bit picky with this style of jacket. If you have a longer torso and shorter legs, know that a slightly cropped version will be more flattering and consider wearing it only with heels in order to balance proportions.

Regardless of how you decide to wear your blazer, make sure it is of good quality. The instant polish part only happens if you buy a good one. Check the quality of the fabric and the construction, and take it to a tailor if the sleeves aren't just right. Check the buttons and the lining too; it should look good with and without the sleeves rolled up. Noted fashion personality Tim Gunn recommends buying well—and thus only having to buy once—in his book *A Guide to Quality, Taste & Style*. "By choosing to spend less on an item you wear all the time, you will ultimately end up spending more as your cheap item requires repairs or replacement."[54]

Black Leather Jacket

There are many styles of leather jackets; buy one that suits your way of life. If you're fairly conservative and you buy a motorcycle style, you probably won't get much use out of it. This is definitely an investment piece, so choose wisely. A great way to cut down on cost is not by compromising but instead by searching for a well-worn vintage one. Whether you're after a *perfecto* or a blazer style, a leather jacket will add that little bit of oomph that makes you feel powerful and edgy.

Trench Coat

Featured in practically every French film ever made, the trench coat is a must when channeling the Parisienne's wardrobe. Any article of clothing that is practical, comfortable, and yet still seen as sexy is a no-brainer. Though trench coats are ubiquitous, they still somehow come across as mysterious, especially when paired with heels and sheer black stockings.

Stick with traditional tan or black, and you'll wear it all the time. Trench coats are fantastic transitional pieces, bridging the gaps between the seasons and acting as an easy coat for spring and fall. Buying one is an absolute must if you live in a rainy climate, because when it's pouring, the trench coat works with everything from gym clothes to formal dresses. If it's not pouring rain or freezing cold, a nice trick is to tie the belt in a knot at the back. This helps define the waistline and adds a bit of polish.

Black Winter Coat

Unless you live in a perennially warm climate and never travel, you'll need a reliable winter coat. A long, classic wool or cashmere version is the most versatile because it works for day or night. Black is the obvious choice because it looks chic, goes with everything, and is the easiest to keep clean (or just appear clean). Thick winter coats can be quite expensive, but there are extremely good values to be had if you shop vintage. I owned one winter coat in my early twenties. It was a wool Neiman Marcus one from the 1960s that I found at a flea market for twenty dollars. I wore it every day when the weather was cold, and it looked and felt fantastic. Just goes to show that good does not need to be expensive. Finding the right item at the right price can take more time, but it will always be worth it.

Stiletto Pumps

The origins of high heels in general are debated, but stiletto heels were invented by Roger Vivier, who worked for Dior at the time. He was able to reinforce the heel to create a slim line, which he called "the needle." Stiletto heels provide instant glamour and sex appeal. They make us carry ourselves differently, which then changes the way we feel and the way others look at us. Stilettos can give you a feeling of power, a sense that you can take on anything, except perhaps a lot of walking. But if you find the right pair in a height that works for you, you'll be surprised at how far you can go in those babies once you break them in. The most practical version of the stiletto is the classic closed-toe pump because it can work year-round for daytime, nighttime, formal events with a dress, or casual events with jeans.

Low- to Midheel Ankle Boots

Spend a little time in Paris and you'll see a ton of ankle booties. The exact style and proportion varies a bit from year to year, but it is definitely a classic staple. You can wear them with jeans or dresses all year around. The Parisienne does. This is where you can vary from black because tan, mahogany, or chocolate-brown boots will look great with a variety of outfits, even all-black ones.

Flats

Obviously every woman needs a great pair of flats. How classic you go is up to you. Ballet flats provide instant femininity, but they can also look too matronly unless styled correctly. Ballet flats are the ideal no-socks-needed shoes. They're good for spring and fall when it's not really cold out but sandals don't feel appropriate. If ballet flats are too classic or too feminine for you, find another flat style that works for you, such as flat boots or sneakers.

K.Jacques Sandals

Buy one pair of tan, flat K.Jacques strappy sandals and wear them all summer long. Tan looks great with black, white, brown, blue, and multicolored outfits, so you can't go wrong. Of course, they don't have to be K.Jacques, but this brand is really worth it. You can buy one pair and wear them for decades. The first few pairs I tried on didn't work for me at all, but once I found my pair, it was love at first sight. I wear them constantly in the summer and on vacation. Just as easy-breezy as flip-flops but far more chic, K.Jacques sandals are made in Saint-Tropez of soft, high-quality leather. They're extremely well made and timeless, and they get more comfortable with time.

Wedge Sandals

In the past, cork was a popular bottom for sandals during wartime because it wasn't a rationed material. Today, cork is a popular choice for wedge sandals because it's light yet sturdy. An even more French-approved version of the wedge is the rope-bottomed version, evocative of the Basque espadrille. Both cork- and rope-bottomed wedges are durable; buy a comfortable pair and wear them for decades. Wedges do go in and out of fashion but are generally considered to be in style in summer. In France, the espadrille wedge sandal is always a summer vacation staple.

Sneakers

Though shunned as too American and too touristy decades ago, sneakers have become a must for Parisiens and Parisiennes. The styles change every couple of years, so some years it will be Converse and some years Adidas Stan Smiths or New Balances, but this is another "worth it" investment because you can wear them all the time. Parisiennes wear them with everything from jeans and T-shirts to black wool trousers and long tailored coats. Just don't wear them with socks (or if you must, buy the kind that don't show).

Leather Handbag for Daytime

Pick one that you can wear every single day and one that suits your lifestyle. Size matters. Be realistic about what you will need to put in it, and keep in mind your frame, body type, and everyday style when choosing a shape. If this is going to be your everyday handbag for a long time, the simpler and less trendy, the better. In many societies, a woman's handbag is a marker of social status. Luckily this is not the case in Paris. If you see a woman with a big Birkin bag dangling from her arm, she is most likely a foreigner. Simple and subtle—and logo-free—handbags are the norm among Parisiennes.

When shopping for a handbag, make sure to steer clear of counterfeits. Though they're tempting if you're on a budget, a Parisienne would never buy counterfeits, and you shouldn't either. Counterfeiters are notorious for employing child labor in horrible conditions. Plus, fashion is the key nonverbal means you have to communicate who you are to the world. Do you really want to tell the world that you're a phony?

I have always been a cost-per-wear girl, never just shopping to shop or buying because something is a bargain, so I personally have never felt the urge to buy counterfeit goods. When I was making twelve dollars per hour as a public relations coordinator in my early twenties, living in a cheap apartment in an unsafe neighborhood, believe me, I was not popping into the nearest luxury store even though I wished I could. During that time, I saved up and bought my handbags on Bluefly.com, an online discount retailer selling out-of-season merchandise. I wore the handbags for years and then ended up consigning them. I definitely came out ahead on the cost-per-wear ratios. Today, sites like TheOutnet.com allow people to buy authentic, high-quality designer clothing and accessories for discount prices and have a good experience doing so. Who cares if it's last season? At least it's real.

Leather Clutch for Nighttime

A small clutch for going out in the evenings is a must because it is not elegant at all to carry around a regular-sized handbag at night. Unless you are coming straight from work, avoid bringing a daytime handbag out to dinner, drinks, or dancing. This seems like a no-brainer, but I've seen a lot of tourists in Paris showing off big, expensive designer handbags at the dinner table. Invest in one good-quality, simple, black, logo-free clutch for nighttime, and you will end up getting a lot of use out of it. It can always be thrown inside your daytime handbag for a desk-to-dinner situation. If shopping online, be careful of the dimensions, making sure that it will fit your phone, keys, lipstick, money, and whatever else you need to carry.

Sheer Black Tights

Other than red lipstick, there are few things more Parisian—or sexier—to wear at night than a pair of sheer black tights. They're slimming, and they'll keep you (slightly) warm, making them ideal for fall and winter evenings. So put on a pair with a little black dress and channel your inner Helmut Newton girl.

If you live in a climate that gets cold in the winter, I would also add a pair of thick black tights to your list, thus making your shorter skirts and dresses pieces that you can wear year-round. This is where it's smart to invest in a high-quality pair because they can last for one year or more without snagging. You can buy one pair of warm wool black tights from Wolford or Falke instead of buying countless far-less-warm and far-less-comfortable pairs that are cheaper but that snag easily.

Scarf

Quintessential for creating the Parisian look and essential for braving a cold winter, a good scarf will keep you warm, comfortable, and polished. Invest in a good black one and keep it for decades. For wool or cashmere winter scarves, I find it easiest to wear them one of two ways, neither of which require lots of skill or practice. The first way is to fold a scarf in half, put it around your neck, and then pull the ends through the loop and adjust. Easy. This works well if you're wearing a coat open in the front and want to protect your neck. The second way is best worn as a finishing piece on top of sweaters and coats: put a scarf around your neck, make sure the two ends are of equal length in front, lightly throw one end over the opposite shoulder, and then repeat with the other end and the other shoulder. Tying scarves can be a bit intimidating, but a quick Google search can show you a variety of ways to tie them.

Le Smoking (Optional)

The first tuxedo for women, "Le Smoking" was designed by my all-time favorite designer, Yves Saint Laurent, as part of his Fall/Winter 1966 collection. Offered to women as an alternative to the little black dress, *le smoking* was incredibly envelope-pushing at the time because it was controversial for women to wear trousers, especially as eveningwear. The legendary American socialite Nan Kempner famously debuted her *le smoking* suit at Le Côte Basque in New York. When she was refused entry into the restaurant for being dressed unsuitably, she removed the pants portion and walked in wearing only the jacket as a micromini. What I wouldn't give to have been in attendance that evening.

Since its debut, *le smoking* has been reworked by the brand many times, but the signature version features a classic black dinner jacket paired with black wool trousers that have a black satin side-stripe. Obviously your version does not need to be Saint Laurent, but make sure to take your suit straight to a tailor so the fit is impeccable. As eveningwear, a woman's version of a man's tuxedo is really a win-win because it's elegant, comfortable, and particularly appropriate for special work events. Due to its illustrious past, it's also inherently feminist and a little rebellious, so you can keep Nan in mind and be feisty and fabulous all evening long.

Chapter 17

Les Femmes Françaises

We can't talk fashion without discussing a few key French (and faux French) fashion icons. It's hard to have a conversation about style icons without bringing up Coco Chanel and Jane Birkin. On the topic of sexpot hair and makeup, Anna Karina and Brigitte Bardot are the poster girls. These women's personal styles are still all over Instagram and Pinterest decades later. They are timeless.

In royal circles, Empress Eugénie and Marie Antoinette forever changed French society as well as the world's view of France. They were strong and determined, and they certainly made their mark. So did pioneers such as Colette and Josephine Baker. Several of these women had less-than-stellar childhoods and spent much of their lives seeking love and admiration. Instead of blending in, they chose to stand out and stand up for themselves and for others.

Quite a few of them were not even born in France, but they became so woven into the fabric of French society that they most certainly count as interesting faux Frenchies. This is by no means a comprehensive listing of the top influential women in France; there are many, many more important women in the country's cultural and political history. I've listed the ones below in an attempt to shed light on a few women who are still holding court in worldwide pop culture. Feel free to dig much deeper, because this list just contains the frosting on top of the cake. That's not to say their stories are boring or shallow—*pas de tout*. Hopefully you will find them just as intriguing as I do.

Anna Karina

This doe-eyed princess of French *nouvelle vague* cinema is best known as being the muse and once-wife of Jean-Luc Godard. But I'm more interested in the fact that she dreamed of Paris from her native home of Denmark, and instead of just dreaming about it, she hitchhiked to Paris at age seventeen all by herself with only 10,000 francs. She has said that she didn't speak a word of French and that she didn't have money to eat for weeks when she arrived, but she found a cheap hotel to stay in near the Bastille, and she made it work. She quickly learned French, and she got her big break while sitting at Les Deux Magots. (See, watching the world go by at a café has its perks.)

She developed a trademark style, including thickly coated mascara and perfectly winged black eyeliner. She became a fashion model, and Coco Chanel helped her devise a new name to use, Anna Karina, instead of Hanne Karin Bayer. Jean-Luc Godard actively sought her out after seeing her in a bubble bath in a Palmolive ad, and she went on to play roles in films such as *Une femme est une femme*, *Vivre sa vie*, *Pierrot le fou*, and *Band of outsiders*. Her relationship to Godard didn't last, but the work they made together is timeless.

Though she was born in Denmark, she became a French citizen. The five-times-married icon has painted, directed, modeled, sung, and written, and she remains a vibrant and mesmerizing fixture on Francophile and vintage social media accounts today. Watch a few of her films (or at least YouTube clips of them), and you'll see why.

Brigitte Bardot

Born in Paris in 1934, Brigitte Anne-Marie Bardot was raised in the bourgeois sixteenth arrondissement by strict parents at home, strict Catholic teachers at school, and strict ballet teachers after school. Every relationship was formal, distant, and very *vous*. As a result, she developed a deep yearning to be loved and to have freedom, two needs that she would carry with her forever.

Though she had successful modeling and acting gigs in her early and middle teen years, she got her big break in the 1952 film *Manina, La fille sans voile* (released in the United States as *Manina, the Girl in the Bikini*), a role that future husband and wild bohemian Roger Vadim helped her land. Her career was certainly helped by her parading around Cannes in her bikini during the 1953 film festival. Vadim, who met Bardot when she was only fourteen years old, taught her about everything from freedom to film to sex, and together they began developing her image as we now freeze it in time today.

While Brigitte was starring in racy films with titles like *Cette sacrée gamine* (released as *Naughty Girl* in the United States), filmmakers in America were bound by strict codes of appropriateness. Marilyn Monroe was barely able to make out on screen during this time. Sexuality in the United States had to be expressed in innuendo only, so you can imagine why Bardot made such a splash. Like a burst of fresh, titillating air, it was not unlike the impact that Vadim had on Bardot after her own rule-filled, love-deprived upbringing.

If the bikini film was her big break, the 1956 megahit *Et Dieu... Créa la femme* (released in the United States as *...And God Created Woman*) was her massive, life-changing break. While apparently seen as a bit ho-hum for French people, the racy film came as a shock to everyone else. It was a huge hit in the United States and England. In Memphis, Philadelphia, and other American cities, some cinema managers were arrested for showing the film, and the Catholic Church tried to have it banned.[55]

"Good people" weren't supposed to watch movies like that, so of course they wanted to. And that they did, in droves. Brigitte Bardot, the blond bombshell, was officially an international star.

The paparazzi and the public became a major problem for Bardot. They mobbed her everywhere she went; she had creepy male fans and stalkers; she had women chastising her for what she represented. So she really never experienced the "real" world as an adult. She hopped from husbands (four) to lovers (many) to movies (many) and then repeated. She did as she pleased, but only in her confined world. She reluctantly had one child, but saying that she lacked maternal instincts, she gave him to her then husband's family to raise.

Bardot retired from her film career at age thirty-nine, well aware of her powerful persona and not wanting to overstay its welcome. She became an avid animal-rights activist, and her extreme right-wing political views (and racist comments about Muslim immigrants in France) have somewhat tarnished her reputation. Though I don't agree with many of her stances, I will always applaud her penchant for staying true to herself and following her passion. Leading a life without regrets is something we should all strive for.

Catherine Deneuve

Born Catherine Dorléac in 1943 to two actors, Catherine Deneuve decided to take her mother's last name, and she began her acting career at age thirteen. Her big break came in the form of the 1964 musical *Les parapluies de Cherbourg* (released in the United States as *The Umbrellas of Cherbourg*). If you haven't seen any Deneuve films, I recommend starting with the weird and wonderful classic

Luis Buñuel film *Belle de Jour,* which is about an uptight bourgeois housewife who decides to become a prostitute in the afternoon to spice up her life.

Catherine Deneuve had high-profile relationships that piqued the public's interest (e.g., Roger Vadim, Marcello Mastroianni, David Bailey), and her classic beauty certainly has a lot to do with her popularity. But above all what strikes me most about Catherine Deneuve is her poise. Whether she is acting a part or living her everyday life, she exudes confidence in a disinterested, unarrogant sort of way. She is cool and calm without ever being stoic.

Though she is internationally famous, most of her films are French. She is a born-and-bred Parisienne who frequently appears around her neighborhood on the *rive gauche,* strolling around Saint-Sulpice or the Jardin du Luxembourg. She is always put together, and she regularly sports the Saint Laurent look, decades after Yves Saint Laurent famously designed her wardrobe for *Belle de Jour.*

Charlotte Rampling

Tessa Charlotte Rampling was born in England, but part of her education took place at a girls' school in Versailles. She began modeling and acting, first appearing in a Cadbury commercial and later getting her big break in a film called *Georgy Girl* in 1966. She went on to make numerous films, including many French ones, and she decided to call Paris home.

Though she has had many professional accomplishments, what is most captivating about her is that feline gaze, which is mesmerizing and a bit haunting. A famous Helmut Newton photograph depicts her posing nude on a table, and though she is naked, her eyes stand out most. This intense stare is present in all of her work and her everyday life, and it is quite Parisienne in the sense that she constantly evokes a sense of mystery. She has had major difficulties in her life, including her sister's suicide, several failed relationships, and even a nervous breakdown at one point. Clearly, there are secrets behind those eyes.

Another Charlotte Rampling trademark is to constantly evolve both her roles and her personal style. In an age where many actresses desperately try to hold on to their youth, she has gone the opposite route, choosing to age *à la française*—confidently and gracefully.

Coco Chanel

Gabrielle "Coco" Chanel had a tough childhood that involved irresponsible parents and a stint at an orphanage, which she would go on to lie about later on in life. She lied about anything and everything, never caring whether her stories corroborated or not. Her upbringing lacked love and security. It also lacked education, worldliness, and material comforts, but she was a sponge, filling in the gaping holes by absorbing the manners and qualities of people she looked up to. She learned whatever she needed to in order to be accepted into a desired social situation, whether it be riding horses or the English language, and she benefited greatly from her ability to think and act like a man. She went from poor little orphan girl to priestess of high society in a time and place where that was no easy feat; perhaps this is why Americans find her life story so appealing.

Her relationships with men were plentiful and complicated. The earlier relationships with wealthy playboys Etienne Balsan and Arthur "Boy" Capel served her well, providing a passport into a glamorous world and the financial backing to start her business. Later relationships with Baron von Dincklage, Grand Duke Dmitri, Paul Iribe, and the Duke of Westminster encouraged her racist, elitist streak.

She was mean-spirited, and she constantly bad-mouthed everyone. She was selfish, unkind to her employees, and extraordinarily racially intolerant. She didn't just sympathize with the Nazis; she collaborated with them. Her personal life was full of shadiness, but her instincts about business were on point. Her discipline, determination, and resourcefulness led to her massive success. By the age of thirty, she had an international business, and she became a multimillionaire before the age of forty. Before the age of fifty, she was worth close to $1 billion in today's currency. Her signature fragrance, Chanel No. 5, is the most successful perfume in history.[56]

She made women feel free by taking away the corset style and creating comfortable and practical clothing for a more athletic lifestyle, but she didn't do it for women's liberation—she did it because that's what suited her boyish body type. She was all in favor of her own liberation as a female but completely uninterested in helping other women succeed. She spent the first couple of decades of her life in poverty but then later looked down upon the poor once she was rich. She didn't just cover her flaws and misfortunes; she turned them into assets and capitalized on them. Even the little black dress came from a period of mourning the death of the love of her life, Boy Capel.

I have read numerous books about Coco Chanel and seen several films and documentaries about her life story. I have toured her elegant apartment on Rue Cambon, complete with the Chanel house codes, including lions, quilting, and camellias. She is an important and inescapable part of the history of fashion and the history of France. She was a visionary, but she was no role model. Of these women, she is the only one I like less the more I learn about her. Her legacy should live on, but it should not be glorified.

Colette

Born in Burgundy, Sidonie-Gabrielle Colette went on to become one of the most influential writers of her time, female or otherwise. Not only was she prolific, turning out numerous pieces of the highest quality, but she also used her work to constantly provoke and break down boundaries. The fact that she chose to go by the name Colette sums up quite a bit about her personality. By dropping her feminine first and middle names and going by her more ambiguous last name, Colette set out to neutralize her gender and play by her own set of rules.

Her sexually frank writing was both shocking and intriguing, as was her own lifestyle. She had many high-profile marriages and relationships; some were with men, and some were with women. It seems that she was born way ahead of her time. Though she published many novels that became famous in France, her most internationally known work is *Gigi*, which went on to become a hit Broadway production and an Academy Award-winning film starring Leslie Caron, Louis Jourdan, and Maurice Chevalier.

Édith Piaf

France's "little sparrow" was born as Édith Gassion in Belleville, a working-class neighborhood of Paris, to a man who loved women and worked in the circus and a woman who loved alcohol and worked as a singer. At one point, she lived with her grandmother, who ran a brothel in Normandy. She was looked after by the prostitutes who lived there, and though she did not grow up with good role models, her childhood provided her with street smarts and the strength of survival. She became a singer on the streets of Paris, which is how she learned to make her voice so powerful, in order to be heard over the din of city life.

She became pregnant at age sixteen and gave birth to a daughter, whom she cared for briefly but then left with the baby's father. The baby died from meningitis at age two, which was the first in a long line of heartbreaks for the singer.

Édith was very unstable and sickly, but she could also be kind and charming. She was teeny, measuring at under five feet tall and at one point weighing as little as sixty-six pounds during one of her many ill periods; that is why her powerful voice was especially surprising. She had stints in rehab and numerous romantic failures, but she also had tremendous professional success. She was so loved by her fans that her funeral procession was at the time the only occasion since World War II to bring Paris traffic to a halt.[57]

She had many admirable qualities beyond her profound stage presence and songwriting ability. She mentored young singers (though admittedly they were usually handsome men who became her lovers), she was overly generous to her numerous friends, and she defied the Nazis by providing shelter and aiding the Resistance. She was constantly falling ill and then making remarkable comebacks, so she became a symbol of resurrection for the French.

Her life was full but also full of sorrows. She made her many mistakes very publicly. This made—and continues to make—her song *"Non, je ne regrette rien"* (which translates to "no, I don't regret anything") especially potent. When Édith Piaf's name is mentioned, it is often in connection with sadness and self-destruction, but when I think of her, I think fondly of this song. Regrets are highly overrated.

Empress Eugénie

María Eugenia Ignacia Augustina Palafox de Guzmán Portocarrero y Kirkpatrick de Closeburn, a.k.a. the Countess of Montijo, would later go on to be known simply as Empress Eugénie. She was born in Spain but grew up mostly in Paris, and by the time she was a young woman, she was a fixture of the high-society scene. When she married Louis-Napoléon, the future Emperor Napoléon III, she was never fully accepted by the Parisians because she was a foreigner. They even booed her on the way to her wedding in the Tuileries, but she stayed true to herself and went on to become influential in many ways.

The emperor and empress brought back extravagant court life to Paris, which was a big change following recent revolutions. The idea was to boost the image of France and its luxury trade. She wore a constant procession of opulent clothing and accessories, never wearing a gown more than once. Her look was emulated all over

Europe. Whenever she wore a new style, such as a cage-crinoline skirt, women in France, England, and the United States adopted the trend within months.

But her influence went far beyond just fashion. She wielded an enormous amount of power, much more than was standard for women in her position at that time. When she played regent in her husband's absence a few times, she thoroughly enjoyed the role. She was passionate, intelligent, and knowledgeable about politics. The empress aided her husband's decisions in all matters, from social issues to foreign affairs.

Though not everyone agreed with all of her political moves, no one can question her legacy of charity work and the advancement of women's rights. She forced the postal service to hire female workers, and she made a woman a member of the much-revered Legion of Honor. She also worked to establish educational systems and rights for girls at a time when female education was considered a waste and a slap in the face of social order. Though the empress led an undoubtedly luxurious lifestyle, she also spent a large portion of her time and money helping others who were unable to help themselves.

Françoise Hardy

Images of sixties-era Françoise Hardy are social media staples these days, because of her authentic Parisienne style and the fact that she is extremely photogenic. She was born in Paris and looks the part. Her marriage to Jacques Dutronc, one of the most celebrated French performers of all time, added to her celebrity allure. In their heyday, they were a power couple in the same vein as Jane Birkin and Serge Gainsbourg.

Françoise Hardy attended the Sorbonne for a year but then dropped out after answering an advertisement calling for singers. She released her first album in 1962, and her sound was perfectly timed with a then popular genre of music called *yé-yé*. This style of pop—derived from the English phrase "yeah! yeah!" (think Beatles)—was big in France, Italy, Spain, and Japan. Other famous counterparts were France Gall and Sylvie Vartan, but Françoise Hardy has really become the international poster girl for the genre.

Jane Birkin

Another French icon born in England, Jane Birkin started her acting career in Swinging Sixties–era London, where she had a few minor film roles. During this time, she was married to English composer John Barry, with whom she had daughter Kate. The marriage did not last long, but Jane was just getting started. Though she didn't really speak French, she went to France to audition for a major role in a film called *Slogan* opposite Serge Gainsbourg. She won both the role and Serge's heart, marking the beginning of her much-celebrated life in France. This was the first of many Jane and Serge collaborations, the most famous of which are their daughter, Charlotte, and the supersexy song *"Je t'aime...moi non plus."*

This stage of Jane Birkin's life is perhaps the one that is most often seen in photographs on social media today. The one constant of her style is its extreme casualness, but during the Serge Gainsbourg era, it was also a bit skimpy and Lolita-like. She wore see-through dresses and teeny-tiny shorts and T-shirts but never a bra. She was photographed often during this time, both by paparazzi and in racy images that she posed for, giving current and future fans a lot of style inspiration to work with. Because her style is so casual, it is a bit ironic that she was the inspiration behind one of the world's fanciest handbags, the Birkin bag. While seated next to Hermès's then chairman and artistic director Jean-Louis Dumas on a flight, Jane told him that she couldn't find a leather bag that suited her lifestyle. He created one for her, and the rest is fabulous fashion history.

She had another daughter, this time with French film director Jacques Doillon. Today, daughters Lou Doillon and Charlotte Gainsbourg are successful singers and actors in their own right. Beyond her famous family, simple-but-powerful personal style, and lengthy singing and acting career, Jane Birkin is also known for her extensive charity work. She has devoted a lot of time to humanitarian efforts, which are a natural fit for a woman with an endlessly positive attitude and such an abundance of love and energy.

Josephine Baker

Josephine MacDonald was born in St. Louis, Missouri, into less-than-ideal conditions; to say that she had an extremely challenging childhood would be an understatement. She grew up sleeping four people to a bed on a bedbug-infested mattress surrounded by rats that her brother Richard used to try to get rid of with a slingshot. As a young girl, she once had to wear the same clothes every day for a year, going barefoot until she was given a castaway pair of high heels that her angry and depressed stepfather cut the heels off of.

She would spend an entire lifetime searching for the love and security her childhood lacked, beginning with her first marriage at age thirteen to Willie Wells, and then her second marriage at age fifteen to Willie Baker. She took this one's last name, becoming Josephine Baker, but then she left him in pursuit of a career on the stage. At age fifteen, she bought a one-way ticket to New York City, and she slept on a bench in Central Park for the first couple of nights.[58]

She found some success in New York and received the opportunity to join a performance troupe in Paris. On the journey to (and subsequent life in) Paris, she and her fellow performers found themselves in a whole new world, one without segregation. Josephine received a lead role in the new production, the highlight of which was a *danse sauvage*, to be performed topless. She became the first star to sing and dance while appearing half-naked. The production opened in October 1925, and fashionable Paris found it shocking and exciting.[59] Josephine became an instant sensation in Paris, and she quickly adapted to life in her new country, changing the spelling of her name to Joséphine. Designers like Madeleine Vionnet showered her with clothing to wear, and men showered her with attention. She went on to have a lengthy singing and dancing career in France, dazzling everyone both onstage and off, wearing glittering gowns and opulent accessories.

Her life was never boring. She adopted twelve children and called them her Rainbow Tribe, and she adopted a cheetah named Chiquita that she paraded down the Champs-Élysées. She also had plenty of personal problems, going through marriages and money at a troubling rate, and she was definitely a diva. But she was also charitable, giving her time and energy to a variety of causes that were close to her heart. She was a pioneer when it came to civil rights, insisting that there had to be black musicians in the house band and no racial discrimination in the sale of tickets when she toured in America. While traveling in the highly segregated South, when she was kicked out of ladies' rooms and lunch counters, she walked right back in.[60] She was a real star—a bright, shining one who will never be forgotten.

Julia Child

Born in Pasadena, California, Julia McWilliams grew to be six feet two inches tall. She was always hungry, and she thought about food constantly. Later, when she relocated to Paris because of husband Paul Child's new post at the American Embassy, she embarked on a six-month training at the renowned Cordon Bleu cooking school. Realizing that she could use her newfound culinary skills for more than just making dinner for her husband, she started working on a cookbook and opened a cooking school with two classmates.

The cookbook turned into what is now considered the French culinary bible in America, the two-volume *Mastering the Art of French Cooking*. The cookbook paved the way for Julia's own television show, *The French Chef*, which was an instant hit. What made her approach so special was her "if I can do it, you can too" attitude, giving her fans the confidence to tackle the intimidating world of French gastronomy.

Julia Child will always hold an important place in the food world because for so many people, she turned home cooking from a necessary chore into a pleasurable passion. She threw herself into a life that was all about French cuisine, and she has inspired many Americans to follow in her footsteps.

Marie Antoinette

I can't think of any other woman in history whose highs were so high and whose lows were so low. Marie Antoinette enjoyed extravagant clothing, over-the-top masked balls, and all-night high-stakes gambling parties. She had a particular weakness for diamonds. But then she became emaciated and severely sick during her later incarceration. She did not die from a swift date with the guillotine; her death was preceded by a long period of suffering. The end of her life was torturous and utterly humiliating.

She married Louis-Auguste, future King Louis XVI, when she was just a teenager. Even though she was born in Austria as an archduchess, Maria Antonia Josefa Johanna had neither a formal education nor the proper preparation for her life as a queen. Perhaps because she was her parents' sixteenth (and last) child, her life at court was not very structured. Given her upbringing and its lack of supervision, along with her husband's social and political clumsiness, her demise was sort of inevitable and not necessarily her fault.

Louis was no help in terms of teaching his wife restraint; his idea of a good breakfast was apparently a whole chicken, four chops, six baked eggs, and some thick ham, all washed down by a bottle and a half of Champagne.[61] The man could eat. Perhaps this would earn him respect at a New York brunch today, but that kind of excess did not go over well during France's long economic depression. Though the queen never said the infamous "let them eat cake" line—that was supposedly said by a previous queen and would have been totally out of character for Marie Antoinette—she did spend wildly for herself and those in her circle at Versailles. The public learned of exactly how much was spent on royal comforts and amusements, and with an unfortunate scandal called the Affair of the Diamond Necklace, Marie Antoinette began her long march toward becoming both the scapegoat and the symbol of the ancient regime.

No matter how hard she tried, she could never please the French. When she acted happily, she was seen as being foolish. When she showed sadness, she was seen as being weak. When she did things simply, they were viewed as improper, but when she ditched her Austrian austerity and adopted the formal luxury of the French court, she was deemed wasteful and frivolous. In the end, she tried to be strong, but the reality is that she was the wife of a weak ruler confronted by a revolution.[62]

There is perhaps no more fitting icon of France than Marie Antoinette. As a foreigner, she was never fully accepted into society. According to biographer Desmond Seward, the French nobility often referred to their queen as *l'Autrichienne,* and they stressed the second half, *chienne* being the word for bitch.[63] The deck was stacked against her, but that is not to say that she had no control in her eventual undoing. For example, long before her beheading, the royal couple left Versailles and moved into the Tuileries in the face of a bankrupt treasury and a starving and impoverished French public. It was a period of rioting, street fighting, and bitterness, but instead of setting up a simple home during such trying times, Marie Antoinette refurbished the Tuileries in the manner of Versailles, complete with elaborate décor and royal rituals. She could have changed course.

Today, she serves as the universal emblem of opulence, and centuries after her death, she is still a regular topic of conversation. For many people, especially foreigners, the Marie Antoinette with her head represents all that is right with France: taste, refinement, and the art of living. For others, especially the French, the headless Marie Antoinette represents all that is right with France: revolutionary ideals, the rejection of excess, and the endless pursuit of an egalitarian utopia that will realistically never come to fruition.

Simone de Beauvoir

A dominant force on the left bank intellectual scene, Simone de Beauvoir published many important works, both fiction and nonfiction. Along with existentialist philosopher and noted Marxist Jean-Paul Sartre, she founded the literary journal *Les Temps modernes*. She and Sartre were partners in work and in love, though their relationship was famously nonmonogamous.

Though she was a feminist, she supported the idea of women being overtly sexual. She strongly emphasized the importance of the individual and of personal choice. She believed that women could become more equal to men via sexual liberation and the ownership of one's body. She also effectively questioned accepted notions of what it meant to be a woman. Asserting that gender was not as biologically prescribed as everyone acted like it was, Simone de Beauvoir believed that women became women through sociocultural conditioning. She was the ultimate feminist existentialist. She was also a *vrai* Parisienne; she was born in Paris, she died in Paris, and she questioned everything.

Chapter 18

Paris, *Je T'Aime*

I f we were to personify Paris, I think most people would think of she, not he. *Elle est belle.* But because I'm American and not French and therefore free to think *à l'extérieur de la boîte,* I've decided that for me, Paris is a man. A handsome Parisien, if you will. Obviously with a five-o'clock shadow, because that's just sexy. But this is your journey too, so feel free to change "he" into "she." (Anyway, we've got to stop our obsession with defining gender, because what's the point? Gender roles are so passé. I swear I'll stop after this one last time.)

It's unhealthy, really, this relationship that I have with him. Just when I think we've made progress, just when I think it's going some-where, I get smacked back into place. There I am minding my own business, and then I see him, and I get sucked right back in. Paris is handsome, after all. And mischievous. And then like clockwork, my mind and my heart race back to the beginning, in tandem, unfortunately.

I see his name in lights like a teenage girl chasing her latest crush does. Every mention of him, every Instagram picture, cuts through the rest so clearly and so powerfully that my heart feels like it stops for a second. And so I go to him. And I go often.

He is a dream. He is a desire. Thankfully, my rational self usually seizes this silliness and points out that we can only desire what we don't possess. Once I lived there full-time, I didn't want him anymore. This reality creeps in on occasion, though not often enough, because the obvious truth doesn't always sit well with our inner cravings, does it? Logic has no place at the negotiating table when it comes to lust and love, so it's back to square one. Or box one, I guess.

I have the utmost admiration for people who can, or who do, last in a country other than their own for more than a couple of years. Everyone's relationship with the motherland is different, and everyone's experience in the new country is different. Some become fully integrated after about a decade, while others resist, guarding their language and their culture by herding with others from their home country. But one thing is the same: it is never easy.

The reality of immigration hit me once while at a medical examination required by the *Office Français de l'Immigration et de l'Intégration*, in which hundreds of people per day are herded through a series of slow-moving lines, crowded waiting areas, and teeny dressing rooms (this part, topless) to be x-rayed and examined by doctors. Though the topless part was certainly no highlight—imagine cold hands and an even colder attitude—it was seeing and hearing other immigrants' stories that made me feel uneasy. Suddenly, love of Haussmannian apartment buildings and a good duck confit no longer seemed like appropriate reasons to abandon my country. The others had real reasons, real struggles. What was I doing there? I had left the land of opportunity, while others had left poverty and persecution in an attempt to find something as basic, and as precious, as freedom.

I would feel like a crazy person if not for the countless Francophiles that I've met along the way. I used to think of my love for Paris as some sort of weird obsession or fetish that I couldn't get enough of. But then this thing called social media flourished, and I met my people. Far from being underground, we're everywhere.

When the topic comes up with others, questions naturally arise: "Why Paris? Why do you love it so much? What draws you in? What is your favorite thing about it?" And when I meet someone who smiles languidly, looks off into the distance, and can't succinctly answer those questions but manages to stumble out some cliché, I know I've found a kindred spirit. This is true love. Blind, unconditional, unexplainable love. And—I think—this is the most special kind.

Because I don't really know either. And yet I wrote a whole book about him. He still eludes me and intrigues me.

He flatters me, and he always stares at me directly in the eyes in a way that I didn't know before but now can't imagine living without. But then he rejects me and he hurts me. Which you would think would push me away. The grass was not greener. Finely groomed and manicured with little signs that indicate you should keep off, yes, but not greener. I should move on, but I can't, and I don't know why. This is basically impossible to explain to French people. Uh, because I'm strangely, magnetically drawn to him? Because he's an irresistible man with irresistible lines, luring me in like stupefyingly willing prey?

But it's really similar to the relationship Parisians have with America—whether they will admit it or not—because they crave a taste of the autonomous life, and they try to recreate it in France whenever possible. It's the freedom to let your freak flag fly. It's wearing jeans. And sneakers. You can be anything you want to be. When rules are made, they are made to be broken. Because in America, looking and acting just like your neighbor is lame.

They're dreaming of cross-country road trips in convertibles, free as birds in their jeans and sneakers and white T-shirts and Ray-Bans listening to American music, headed to the Wild West. Whether that's a reference to horse-riding cowboys or Internet entrepreneurs is generational, but the point is the same: *Li-ber-té*. The all-encompassing kind.

Partial to both cowboys and Internet entrepreneurs, and the lack of unbreakable boxes and irrational rules, the United States of America—and more specifically, New York—is and always will be the place for me. But Paris will forever be a part of my life, albeit in a supporting role and not the starring one. I'm glad I got out when I did, before things turned routine. Perhaps that's best. I can admire him from afar and see him in person occasionally. New York is my best friend, the one I can always count on to entertain me, to support me, and above all, to love me. I pined for Paris for so long. Then I had him. Then I lost him. But now I've learned to accept our fate. Instead, I can just sit back and enjoy desire for desire's sake. Perhaps for eternity.

We'll Always Have Paris

A few years into my life in New York, in my New York—the one I've created for myself that's overwhelmingly French but not in France—something happened to me that completely changed my perspective on life. One night at an after party following a great party, where my husband and I were as usual two of very few Americans and where English was not the default language, a couple of French women did something mean to me in a grand effort to make fun of what I was wearing. I ranted and raved about it for the next few days, and I went through phases of feeling mad, stupid, and left out.

But then something wonderful happened: for the first time in my life, I realized that all I could do was be myself. I could never please them, nor did I want to. I don't know why it took some silly French women to make me see this and feel empowered, but it did. And life has never been better. It's a beautiful thing to embrace yourself and be proud of who you are. I think it's the secret to a great life, and if you don't currently feel like this, please don't wait until someone else shakes you up to become your strongest, best self. Do it now, because it's so liberating.

In order to figure out what this best self is, sometimes it's helpful to explore other cultures and study other people. Yes, we could be ourselves and stay in a bubble, but that doesn't benefit anyone. There's something special about taking a look at other cultures and borrowing bits and pieces; it makes the world feel like a more intimate, more familiar, and friendlier place, and we could all use a bit of that.

There are so many gifts I've received from being faux French: enjoying good food and a (finally) healthy relationship with my body, going out and having fun, embracing getting older, and having a more global perspective. But most importantly, I gained confidence.

Identify what you feel you're lacking in life. What do you want more or less of? Then find a culture that's known for that and *Eat, Pray, Love* your way in or out of whatever you desire. But you don't even need to leave home to "travel." Through books, films, food, and social media, you can travel with your eyes and your mind, and you can find the piece that's eluding you. I thought I wanted a little more sophistication in my life, so I turned to Paris, but what I found instead was my own sense of self. So I wish you the best of luck on your journey of self-discovery.

Bon courage et bon voyage!

Appendix A

Fun French Facts

France is a country full of formality and passion—and contradictions. Gestures or habits that seem simple are often full of complexity and backstories. Life in Paris is ordered chaos, with lots of baggage. France as a country—and France as a concept—is difficult to summarize, but piecing together little tidbits from the past and the present is a fun place to start.

- Thomas Jefferson—considered by many to be America's first Francophile—had eighty-six packing crates shipped back home to the States from Paris. Among the many kitchen utensils, fabrics, and pieces of furniture, he also brought back Champagne, french fries, and the recipe for crème brûlée.[64]

- France is home to the world's first filmmakers, the Lumière brothers. They invented the *cinématographe*, which allowed simultaneous viewers to watch projections together, and their film *Sortie de l'usine Lumière de Lyon* (1895) is considered to be the first motion picture. This film was part of the first public film screening in which admission was charged, held in 1895 in Paris.

- Perfume is not just for Parisiennes. The agency that runs the Paris subway system is called the RATP, and it perfumes the subway in order to neutralize the unfavorable smells that are an inevitable part of urban transportation. In the 1990s, the RATP tried out a perfume called Francine, which was a mixture of natural plant extracts, but it failed in trials. They found a winner in a scent called Madeleine, which is a synthetic mix of vanilla, jasmine, lily, citrus, and rose. Since 1998, the RATP has poured 1.5 metric tons of Madeleine onto subway stations per month.[65]

- The modern striptease is said to have been created in Paris in the 1890s in a music hall on the right bank. A woman named Blanche Cavelli, playing the famous cabaret artist Yvette Guilbert, undressed onstage as she got ready for bed. The skit was called "Yvette's Going to Bed," and it became so popular that it inspired at least thirty similar skits in Paris.[66]

- Fashion as we know it really began with an English tailor, named Charles Frederick Worth, who practiced in Paris. In the 1850s, Worth opened his own couture house, and he was really the first fashion designer in that he designed clothing and clients came to buy his designs. Previously, clients had dictated the designs they wanted, and the tailors and dressmakers simply had executed their clients' wishes. But Worth turned the profession on its head, elevating himself from merely a dressmaker into an *haute couturier*, creating lavish gowns for clients. He was the first in the industry to really understand the importance of branding, and he made sure his name was on the labels of his dresses and on the lips of his famous clients. He held fashion shows at the House of Worth, complete with live models, which was a first. Clients selected the designs they liked, and Worth created one-of-a-kind pieces for them based upon the models, similar to the *haute couture* system of today.

- *La rentrée*—the reentry in September after the summer holiday—is a wonderful time to be in France. After a summer (or at least a few weeks) apart from each other, friends get together and catch up about each other's *vacances*. Everyone is in town during September, tanned and happy. It is probably the one time in Paris when you'll catch everyone smiling and acting all carefree, actually expressing excitement upon seeing each other. Children are reunited with their friends again, and they seem happy to be heading off to school, for this month, anyway. There are nonstop events and lunches and dinners and parties, and it feels like a fun, fresh start to a new year. I used to think of New Year's Day as the start to each new year, a time to reflect, rejoice, and look forward, but now *la rentrée* has taken its place.

- Prior to the birth of French *haute cuisine*, sweet dishes were part of every course. In this new form of cooking, French chefs allowed salt and pepper to dominate until the end of the meal. Sweet dishes were gradually moved to the last course, called *le dessert*.[67]

- Very few French foods are actually from Paris, with most items on Parisian menus being specialties of other regions (e.g., a lardons salad with poached eggs is from Lyon, ratatouille is from Provence, and clafoutis is from Limousin). But certain mushrooms, namely *champignons de Paris*, were historically cultivated in the city's former catacombs, which offered darkness, humidity, and constant temperatures. With only a couple producers left working just outside of Paris, the legitimate local version is rare but fascinating nonetheless.

- Montmartre used to be outside the city limits of Paris. Originally a rural village dotted with windmills and vineyards, Montmartre (and its thirty-three thousand residents) wasn't officially annexed into the city until the mid-1800s.

- The Place des Vosges on the *rive droite* was the original modern city square and the first space in any European capital built simply for recreational use. The area around the Place des Vosges was called the Marais, which became the original example of an upscale Parisian neighborhood.[68]

- I used to cross the Pont Neuf in Paris and assume that it was the ninth bridge, which was far from correct. It actually means "new bridge," and it played a key role in making Paris into the Paris that we know today. It introduced Parisians to a new kind of street life, and it became the heart of the city, connecting the right bank to the left without the need for a boat. It was the first bridge whose entire surface was paved, and it even featured sidewalks, which encouraged people to cross on foot. It is now the oldest bridge in Paris, still going strong because it was built of stone instead of wood and is thus fireproof.[69]

- The Île Saint-Louis—that mostly man-made island in the middle of the city, in the Seine—holds a special place in the hearts of Parisians and tourists alike. The project to turn what was basically nothing into one of the city's most elegant neighborhoods was executed by Louis XIII, who was carrying out the plans of his father, Henri IV. It was completed in

1640, and its layout and architecture still look much the same today.[70]

- Though the Statue of Liberty is very much associated with what it means to be an American, it was actually a gift from the French. It was designed by French sculptor Frédéric Auguste Bartholdi and built by Gustave Eiffel.

- The connection between New Orleans and France is well-known, but I had forgotten just how much of the United States was involved in the Louisiana Purchase. The *Vente de la Louisiane* was the sale of 828,000 square miles of land in 1803 from the French government to the US government. It included land from two Canadian provinces and fifteen present-day states: Arkansas, Colorado, Iowa, Kansas, Louisiana, Minnesota, Missouri, Montana, Nebraska, New Mexico, North Dakota, Oklahoma, South Dakota, Texas, and Wyoming.

- The infamous guillotine all began with a man named Dr. Guillotin, who was opposed to the current state of capital punishment, despising the way it had become a public spectacle. Crowds of people—including children—gathered to watch felons be hacked to death or burned at the stake. But that was for the poor ones. Meanwhile, wealthy felons often bribed the executioner to drug them first or sometimes kill someone in their place. Dr. Guillotin felt that every criminal should be killed in the same way, whether rich or poor. The National Assembly agreed and put him on a committee to solve the problem. The solution was found in Tobias Schmidt, maker of harpsichords, who created a prototype of a decapitation device for the committee. The device was a hit, but ultimately too much of one, because every town in France wanted one, and the public death spectacles continued until 1939. Many people (especially foreigners) associated Dr.

Guillotin with the device and began calling it "Madame la Guillotine." Two families, the Sansons and the Deiblers, performed every execution between 1792 and 1977. The executioner, always called "Monsieur de Paris," had the right to *tutoyer* the prisoner, addressing him informally as *tu*, not the formal *vous*.[71]

Appendix B

Ready to (Mentally) Travel to Paris?

Films

Some of these selections won't get you brownie points among French film buffs, but life isn't all *nouvelle vague*, you know? Though I love Godard and Truffaut, sometimes it's nice to watch something silly or romantic (or better yet, both), especially if you're relying on subtitles. The films from the list below are widely available on iTunes, Amazon, or Netflix and are sure to please any faux Frenchie. I've listed them by the titles they were released under in the United States. If you have any recommendations for me, I'd love to hear them (e-mail: jordan@lureofluxe.com, Twitter: @ jphillipsNY, Instagram: @inspiredbyparis).

- *2 Days in Paris* (2007): French photographer Marion (Julie Delpy) and American interior designer Jack (Adam Goldberg) attempt to add some romance into their relationship by taking a trip to Paris. If you like Julie Delpy's frenetic speaking style, you will enjoy this film.

- *8 Women* (2002): A silly murder mystery musical, this film is worth watching just for the all-star cast alone: Catherine Deneuve, Isabelle Huppert, Fanny Ardant, Emmanuelle Béart, and Virginie Ledoyen.

- *Amélie* (2001): Probably the first film every Francophile-to-be watches, this one tracks the life of a quirky, shy Parisienne who is determined to execute her own sense of justice. Audrey Tautou is at her most charming. This film won international praise and was nominated for five Academy Awards, including best original screenplay.

- *An American in Paris* (1951): Certainly watch this musical before you see it on Broadway. In this film, starring Gene Kelly and Leslie Caron, an American artist struggling to find work in Paris is torn between a French dancer and a wealthy American woman. It was the winner of six Oscars, including best picture.

- *...And God Created Woman* (1956): It's a revolutionary Roger Vadim film set in Saint-Tropez starring Brigitte Bardot, so definitely see this one.

- *April in Paris* (1952): A chorus girl mistakenly receives an invitation from the US government to represent American theater at a cultural junket in Paris, and an unlikely romance begins. Starring Doris Day, this lively film is filled with glamorous costumes and Champagne-fueled dance sequences.

- *A Woman Is a Woman* (1961): The basic storyline is that an exotic dancer is desperate to have a child with her boyfriend, but when he says no, she turns to his best friend. Naturally, things get complicated. Directed by Jean-Luc Godard, this classic *nouvelle vague* film stars the captivating Anna Karina and the irresistible Jean-Paul Belmondo.

- *Before Sunrise* (1995), *Before Sunset* (2004), and *Before Midnight* (2013): This trio of films—shot over the course of decades—chronicles the relationship of an American guy named Jesse and a French girl named Céline, played by Ethan Hawke and Julie Delpy. The films are about romance, love, and family, and about coming to terms with the past, present, and future.

- *Belle de Jour* (1967): This surreal, erotic film starring Catherine Deneuve is a must watch for any Francophile. It tracks a distant and aloof upper-middle-class Paris housewife as she secretly starts working as a prostitute. Don't miss the fantastic fashion by Yves Saint Laurent.

- *Beloved* (2011): This odd yet captivating film follows the sordid love lives of two women, played by Catherine Deneuve and her real-life daughter, Chiara Mastroianni.

- *Bonjour Tristesse* (1958): Jean Seberg stars in this beautiful film about complicated relationships, based on the novel by Françoise Sagan. Though the setting is in the French Riviera, the dialogue is in English. I guarantee you'll rethink your summer wardrobe after seeing Seberg's chic but effortless ensembles.

- *Breathless* (1960): The first time I started watching this, I turned it off because the beginning was so weird. But years later, I tried again, and it is now one of my favorite films. Yes, it's weird, but gloriously so. Directed by Jean-Luc Godard and written by François Truffaut—the ultimate *nouvelle vague* duo—this film was a game changer at the time, and it still dazzles today. A cute and quirky Jean Seberg plays an American in Paris who's fallen for a bad boy (a real one, the stealing and killing kind), played to perfection by Jean-Paul Belmondo. Add it to your watch list immediately!

- *Chinese Puzzle* (2013): It helps to watch *The Spanish Apartment/ L'auberge espagnole* before watching this, but it isn't required. Featuring the same cast (including Audrey Tautou and Romain Duris), only older, it is about family, life, love, and relocation.

- *Chocolat* (2000): It's a film about chocolate set in France, and it features Johnny Depp...need I say more?

- *Contempt* (1963): The thing that I love most about Jean-Luc Godard films is that they sit with you for a while; watch one and it will creep in and out of your consciousness for the next few weeks. This one, starring Brigitte Bardot, has become one of my favorites. It's slow-paced but full of nudity, arguments, and jaw-dropping scenery.

- *Day for Night* (1973): A delightful film about the making of films, it is filled with industry insider information and awesome 1970s fashion. The whole thing takes place behind the scenes, so you get to see how movies are made and how the lines between personal and professional are blurred during filming. Jacqueline Bisset is positively radiant playing Julie Baker, a British actress fresh out of a nervous breakdown. This is a must watch for fans of Truffaut, who not only wrote and directed this film but also stars in it.

- *Funny Face* (1957): Audrey Hepburn and Fred Astaire star in this classic Gershwin musical set in Paris. If you love fashion, the Edith Head–designed costumes are not to be missed.

- *Gigi* (1958): Based on a novella by the famous French writer Colette, *Gigi* is a delightful film starring Leslie Caron, Louis Jourdan, and Maurice Chevalier. This one checks a lot of boxes: it's a musical without really being a musical (no long, drawn-out song-and-dance sequences), and it's a film about France set in Paris, but it's all in English. It's fun for everyone.

- *Girl on a Bicycle* (2013): This quirky film follows the romantic mishaps of Paolo, an Italian who drives a tour bus. It's a silly, and a bit preposterous, romantic comedy, but it's good for anyone looking for a lighthearted film set in Paris.

- *Heartbreaker* (2010): I absolutely love *Heartbreaker*, known in France as *L'Arnacoeur*. It is one of those romantic comedies that you can watch again and again. Romain Duris plays Alex, who is hired to break up relationships that friends and family members don't approve of. His sidekicks are his sister and her husband, played by the hilarious Julie Ferrier and François Damiens, and their current assignment is to break up the impending marriage of Juliette (Vanessa Paradis). Be prepared to laugh, cry, and fall in love with *L'Arnacoeur*. Romain Duris and Vanessa Paradis's re-creation of that famous scene from *Dirty Dancing* is swoonworthy.

- *How to Steal a Million* (1966): Audrey Hepburn and Peter O'Toole star in this classic caper set in Paris. Audrey Hepburn plays a woman who must steal a statue from a museum in order to help conceal her father's art forgeries.

- *Jefferson in Paris* (1995): Nick Nolte plays America's first Francophile, Thomas Jefferson, in this historical drama. Though a bit slow at times, it's worth watching for a bit of context surrounding his role as the American Ambassador to France from 1784 to 1789.

- *Jules and Jim* (1962): Weird and wonderful, *Jules et Jim* follows the whims of the crazy and passionate Catherine, played by Jeanne Moreau, and her never-ending quest for attention. Truffaut wrote the film adaptation and directed this enchanting story of a love triangle.

- *La chèvre* (1981): A young Gérard Depardieu stars in this slapstick comedy about a French businessman who sends his accident-prone accountant to search for his accident-prone daughter who is lost in Mexico.

- *Le Divorce* (2003): Based on the novel by Diane Johnson, this film stars Kate Hudson and Naomi Watts, who play sisters learning about and adapting to French customs. I thoroughly enjoyed both the book and the film adaptation.

- *La Moustache* (2005): This psychological mystery starts off with a simple enough storyline, with a French architect named Marc who decides to shave off his mustache. When no one notices that he's suddenly shaved it off, he begins pressing friends and family about it. Things get complicated when they all insist that he hasn't had a mustache in years.

- *La Vie en Rose* (2007): Marion Cotillard brilliantly plays French *chanteuse* Édith Piaf, whose private life was tragic but whose songs continue to inspire many.

- *Le Chef* (2012): If you're interested in fine dining and movies about food, this is a good one. It's about a renowned older chef who finds an opponent in his restaurant group's new CEO, who wants to bring in a younger chef who specializes in molecular gastronomy.

- *Le Week-End* (2013): An older British couple revisits Paris for the first time since their honeymoon in an attempt to rejuvenate their marriage.

- *Little White Lies* (2012): When a group of friends goes on a summer vacation together, little secrets and personal problems are revealed. Directed and written by the talented Guillaume Canet, *Les petits mouchoirs* features an all-star cast including Marion Cotillard, François Cluzet, and Jean Dujardin. It is an ideal film to watch if you're interested in learning more about the intricacies of the French because it offers a realistic portrayal of typical relationship dynamics and cultural norms.

- *Made in Paris* (1966): A dazzling Ann-Margret plays a fashion buyer headed to Paris on her first buying trip. Once in the French capital, she finds plenty of adventure and plenty of men. This classic film is a must watch for the fabulous fashion and fun dance scenes alone.

- *Marie Antoinette* (2006): Kirsten Dunst plays Marie Antoinette in this Sofia Coppola production, which begins with her marriage to Louis XVI and covers the hard-partying, macaron-and-Champagne-filled years that follow.

- *Midnight in Paris* (2011): Paris loves Woody Allen, and apparently Woody Allen now loves Paris. A nostalgic screenwriter (played by Owen Wilson) goes on walks at night in the City of Light and ends up traveling through time.

- *Mississippi Mermaid* (1969): A trippy Truffaut film starring Catherine Deneuve and Jean-Paul Belmondo, *Mississippi Mermaid* is about a tobacco planter on Reunion Island and his mail-order bride. Only the French can combine romance, crime, and drama so seamlessly.

- *Moulin Rouge* (2001): I'm guessing you've already seen this dazzling, high-octane Baz Luhrmann spectacle, but I think you're due for a rewatch. Starring Nicole Kidman, Ewan McGregor, John Leguizamo, and a whole host of addicting songs, we learn about the Bohemian ideals of truth, beauty, freedom, and, above all things, love. The courtesan Satine learns that diamonds are not a girl's best friend, because "the greatest thing you'll ever learn is just to love and be loved in return." The entire production is, in the words of Harold Zidler, "a magnificent, opulent, tremendous, stupendous, gargantuan, bedazzlement, a sensual ravishment."

- *My Best Friend* (2006): Starring Daniel Auteuil and Dany Boon (two excellent actors), this is the story of an acrimonious man who is challenged to prove that he is likeable. He has ten days to make a friend but learns that true friendship is hard to find.

- *Paris* (2008): Juliette Binoche and Romain Duris star in this touching film about a man who suffers from a serious heart disease but discovers the little joys of life in Paris.

- *Paris, I Love You* (2006): An absolute must see for any Francophile, *Paris, je t'aime* is a collection of eighteen short films set in Paris, all of which surprise and delight.

- *Paris When It Sizzles* (1964): Audrey Hepburn plays an assistant to a Hollywood screenwriter (William Holden) and helps him overcome writer's block by acting out various plot scenarios.

- *Picture Paris* (2012): This short film (twenty-nine minutes) stars Julia Louis-Dreyfus as an American woman obsessed with all things French. She plans the trip of a lifetime to Paris, but things don't turn out as planned. The end is definitely surprising...just don't watch it with children around.

- *Populaire* (2012): Romain Duris stars in this supercute film about a typing competition in 1958. The premise is silly, but it's a quirky, fun, and lovable film.

- *Priceless* (2006): A young gold digger (played by Audrey Tautou) looking for a wealthy suitor on the French Riviera mistakes a bartender (Gad Elmaleh) for her target. It's sort of a French version of *Breakfast at Tiffany's*.

- *Quantum Love* (2014): I'm completely obsessed with this romantic film featuring Sophie Marceau and François Cluzet, who play two people who cannot seem to shake their mutual attraction for each other. It has shades of *Sliding Doors* but with a French twist.

- *Romantics Anonymous* (2010): An awkward man and an extremely timid woman are united through their passion for chocolate.

- *Sabrina* (1954): The film was remade in 1995, but the original Audrey Hepburn version is far better. It features an adorable coming-of-age tale about a playboy who falls in love with his chauffeur's daughter but only after she returns emerged as a butterfly following a stint in Paris.

- *The Closet* (2001): So funny, so not politically correct, so French. If you are easily offended, this is not the film for you. But the French are not at all politically correct, so this is a good intro to the cultural mind-set. The characters played by Gérard Depardieu, Danny Auteuil, and Thierry Lhermitte prove that little white lies are not always so little but are definitely hilarious.

- *The Dinner Game* (1998): In order to amuse themselves at regular dinner parties, a group of French guys invites unsuspecting idiots, or *cons,* and pretends to be friends with them. Whoever invites the biggest idiot wins. Though even less politically correct than *The Closet,* this film is just as funny.

- *The Diving Bell and the Butterfly* (2007): So sad, so good. Based on a true story, this film is about a journalist who is paralyzed by a stroke but finds a way to communicate.

- *The Gilded Cage* (2013): This is a beautiful yet lighthearted film about Portuguese immigrants working and living in Paris.

- *The Intouchables* (2011): I cannot praise this film with François Cluzet and Omar Sy highly enough. You'll laugh, you'll cry, and you'll appreciate everything in life. A must watch for Francophiles and non-Francophiles alike.

- *The Last Metro* (1980): This powerful Truffaut film is about an actress (played by Catherine Deneuve) who is married to a Jewish theater owner and her quest to hide him in occupied wartime Paris.

- *The Last Time I Saw Paris* (1954): Starring Elizabeth Taylor, this film chronicles the rollercoaster love life of an American couple in Paris.

- *The Soft Skin* (1964): This is a classic French film about an affair but with a nonclassic Truffaut ending.

- *The Spanish Apartment* (2002): A French student (played by Romain Duris) moves into an apartment in Barcelona with a group of other Europeans, and his view on life changes forever after living in such an international environment.

- *The Swimming Pool* (1969): Starring Alain Delon, Romy Schneider, and Jane Birkin, this not-to-be-missed cult classic addresses typically French topics like summer vacation, sexual tension, and jealousy.

- *The Umbrellas of Cherbourg* (1964): I do love a good musical, but this film is all musical, meaning that every single word is sung. It's certainly not for everyone, but it's a great tool for anyone who is learning French because the entire thing comprises simple phrases sung slowly and clearly. Paired with subtitles, it's quite helpful for learning some phrases or refreshing your French. Plus, it stars Catherine Deneuve.

- *The Valet* (2006): This goofy film featuring Gad Elmaleh and Daniel Auteuil is about a regular guy who gets caught up in the love life of a billionaire and his model mistress. It's cheesy but in a good way.

- *The Young Girls of Rochefort* (1967): I can only recommend this one to people who either really love musicals or are hardcore Francophiles. Or to children; my daughter loves it. Like *Les parapluies de Cherbourg*, this film features brightly colored clothing and backdrops and an easy-to-follow plotline, as well as Catherine Deneuve. It also stars Deneuve's real-life sister Françoise (who died tragically in 1967 in a car accident in the South of France).

- *What's in a Name* (2012): Totally weird, totally French, *What's in a Name* is a fantastic film about a simple subject that turns into something darker.

- *Young & Beautiful* (2013): This sexy and scandalous film is about a beautiful young girl who decides to be a prostitute despite having no need for making extra money. It's sort of a modern-day version of *Belle de jour*.

Pinterest Accounts

There's something about seeing images of Paris and typically Parisian things—no matter how ubiquitous—that makes me instantly feel a rush of happiness. Just seeing a stack of macarons in my feed makes me smile. It's not about the taste alone; it's the *idea* of the macarons, those little jewels of food perfection, that makes me feel good. They represent indulgence, luxury, and sophistication, like the sound of a Champagne cork popping. Just looking at them can transport me to another place, if even for a second. To find some good Parisian things to follow, go to the search box on Pinterest and type in "macarons" or "Paris" or "France" or "Yves Saint Laurent" or whatever you'd like, and then click on the Boards button and begin following whatever looks promising. Your feed will soon be filled with French things.

Instagram Accounts

I really enjoy "traveling" via Instagram. While sometimes scrolling through your feed might make you feel like everyone else's life is more fantastic than yours, it's helpful to remember that people are often posting only the highlights, so it's not necessarily an accurate portrayal of everyday life. Instead of just following along by checking in on your feed and posting pictures, it can also be fun to search for things you're interested in and find new images and new ideas from people you don't even know.

For example, if your feed is accosted by pictures of an ex-boyfriend gallivanting around Paris with his new girlfriend, that's probably not going to make you feel very good. But if you're searching through strangers' virtual postcards from Paris, that can be entertaining and informative. You can find out about new music to listen to or get inspiration for decorating, cooking, or new ways to tie a scarf. You can observe street styles and trends from around the world without even leaving home. Or find other Francophiles within your own city via Instagram and see what they're up to, perhaps learning about a new French bistro in your neighborhood. Here are some fantastic Francophile accounts that I follow. No passport required.

- Alina Kolot: @alinakolot
- Anastasiya Lapina: @lapina_colada
- Angeline Melin: @angelinemelin
- Anna Cossack: @annacossack
- Arthur Gosse: @arthur_gosse
- Avecmar: @avecmar
- Brandie Raasch: @brandieraasch
- Brigitte Bardot BB: @brigittebardotbb
- Carin Olsson: @parisinfourmonths
- Carrie Anne James: @frenchisbeautiful
- Catherine Deneuve Daily: @catherinedeneuvedaily
- Cedric Grolet: @cedricgrolet
- Chateau de Versailles: @chateauversailles
- Chris Bell: @chrissen
- Cris: @crissilveira
- Do It in Paris: @doitin_paris
- Elie: @elieyobeid

- Faustine Poidevin: @faustpdv

- Francoise Hardy Daily: @francoisehardydaily

- Frank Adrian: @cakeboyparis

- French Words: @frenchwords

- French Words Journal: @frenchwordsjournal

- Guillaume Dutreix: @guillaume_dx

- Haleigh Chastain Walsworth: @byhaleigh

- Hana Predajnianska: @journeyintolavillelumiere

- Inspired by Paris: @inspiredbyparis

- Jane Birkin Daily: @janebirkindaily

- Jeanne Damas: @jeannedamas

- Juan Jerez: @juanjerez

- Le Mec Qui Clique: @lemecquiclique

- Love French Movies: @lovefrenchmovies

- Marissa Cox: @ruerodier

- Merrit: @beaubonjoli

- Nouvelle Vague: @nouvellevaguefr

- Paolo: @freepy

- Rapius: @paris_by_rapius

- Sam J: @callicles

- Saul Aguilar: @saaggo

- Spiritual Walker: @spiritualwalker

- Studio 6lettres: @6lettres

- Top Paris Photo: @topparisphoto

- Vis Paris: @visparis

Books

Reading about Paris can sometimes be more rewarding than watching films because your mind can create the scenery. Below are some of my favorite books for learning and dreaming about all things French.

- *A Paris Apartment,* by Michelle Gable: This historical novel is set in modern-day Paris and simultaneously the Belle Époque. It has an addictive I-must-find-out-what-happens-next-even-though-it's-2:00-a.m. quality, and it is the perfect combination of light and informative. You'll learn a little history all while guessing who is going to do what with which love interests.

- *Au Bonheur des Dames,* by Émile Zola: A fictional version of the very real story of the famed department store Le Bon Marché on Paris's *rive gauche* in the mid-1800s, this novel is ideal for anyone who loves reading about fashion history. If you enjoy the book, I suggest watching BBC's "The Paradise" series on Netflix. It is set in England but has a similar story line.

- *Bright Lights Paris: Shop, Dine, and Live...Parisian Style,* by Angie Niles: This is a comprehensive guidebook for where to go in Paris, particularly if you love food. Broken down by neighborhood (and style), *Bright Lights Paris* is a handy companion for your next visit to the City of Light.

- *Brigitte Bardot: Liberté,* by Danny Lewis: If you're a Bardot fan, this book is a must. It's a quick, concise read that covers all of the basics that you'd want to know about her, including her good qualities (determination) and her bad (racism). Though short on length, it's not short on insight or intelligence. While reading about Bardot's later-life political leanings always makes me wince, I'm enamored by her lifelong assertion to stay true to herself and do as she pleases, regardless of consequence. The book provides an accurate, but not unflattering, portrayal of this inimitable bombshell.

- *How to Be Parisian Wherever You Are*, by Anne Berest, Audrey Diwan, Caroline de Maigret, and Sophie Mas: If you want to better understand how Parisiennes think, read this book. It's fun, informative, and full of deliciously quotable bon mots.

- *La Seduction: How the French Play the Game of Life*, by Elaine Sciolino: Written by a longtime American expat who lives in Paris, *La Seduction* is more scholarly and politically minded than I would expect for a book about seduction, but I loved every word. It's a great balance between informative and fun, especially for anyone who's interested in the Paris scene or politics in general.

- *Lunch in Paris*, by Elizabeth Bard: This is one of the few books that accurately describe what it's like to live in Paris. The real version, not the Instagram one. *Lunch in Paris* is an honest and highly personal account of a New Yorker turned Parisienne adopting a new home country in the name of love.

- *Mastering the Art of French Eating: From Paris Bistros to Farmhouse Kitchens, Lessons in Food and Love*, by Ann Mah: When Ann Mah's diplomat husband is given a three-year assignment in Paris, she is overjoyed. But not long after the couple's relocation, her husband is reassigned to Iraq for a year, so she is left to adapt to living in Paris alone. *Mastering the Art of French Eating* is an intelligent and interesting book sure to please any food-loving Francophile.

- *Naughty Paris: A Lady's Guide to the Sexy City,* by Heather Stimmler-Hall: If you're open-minded and ready for a little reading adventure, this guidebook fits the bill. Offering advice on milder topics like lingerie and more advanced topics like where to find a good sex club in Paris, Heather Stimmler-Hall is extremely knowledgeable about all things Paris and all things racy.

- *Paris, I Love You but You're Bringing Me Down,* by Rosecrans Baldwin: This one is a witty and accurate portrayal of what it's like to move to Paris from the United States (in his case, New York) without a firm grasp of the French language. Naturally, mishaps occur. The title alone sums up many an expat Parisian experience. Whether or not you're contemplating a long-term stay in Paris, you'll certainly find it entertaining.

- *Parisian Chic: A Style Guide by Inès de la Fressange,* by Inès de la Fressange and Sophie Gachet: This fashion-and-style-focused how-to book is a breezy read that's perfect for women wanting to revamp their wardrobes in order to achieve a more classically polished Parisian look.

- *Picnic in Provence,* by Elizabeth Bard: This beautifully written book will make you want to hop on the next plane to Provence. If you love food and books about France, this book is a must read. Elizabeth Bard provides lots of delicious recipes, several of which have become new favorites in my home.

- *Stuff Parisians Like: Discovering the Quoi in the Je Ne Sais Quoi,* by Olivier Magny: This is hands down my favorite book about Paris. The witty and in-the-know Olivier Magny hilariously describes the nuances of Parisians. I wish I had read this before moving there.

.

Ready to (Physically) Travel to Paris?

Visiting Paris 101

Whether you're planning your first visit to Paris or your first visit in a long time, I think you'll find the below tips quite helpful. They are all things that I wish I would have known before my first visit.

- Postal codes let you know the arrondissement, so for example, if a restaurant's address is 6 rue Perronet, 75007 Paris, you know it's in the seventh arrondissement. If the address is 8 rue des Ciseaux, 75006 Paris, you know it's in the sixth.

- Fun, tourist-friendly streets to explore are Rue du Bac and Rue Cler in the seventh, Rue de Buci and Rue du Cherche-Midi in the sixth, Rue Saint-Honoré in the first and eighth, Rue Montorgueil in the second, and walks along the Seine and Canal Saint-Martin. For something slightly less tourist friendly but more authentic, try Rue des Martyrs in the ninth. It offers every sort of food product you could ever want, so it's a great street to seek out if you're renting an apartment in Paris and plan on eating in. It's also a nice add-on stop if you're already going to the Montmartre area. On rainy days, nice "streets" to explore are three adjacent *passages*, or covered walkways: Passage Verdeau, Passage Jouffroy, and Passage des Panoramas. Passage Jouffroy is a bit lackluster, but it bridges the other two. Passage des Panoramas is a fantastic spot to eat lunch or dinner, offering a wonderful mix of old-school authentic places and newer hipster places. To me, the Passage des Panoramas sums up so much of what I love about Paris because it's a spot that's steeped in history and is welcoming to both foreigners and locals alike. It represents the new and the old.

- The Eiffel Tower (*la Tour Eiffel*) sparkles for five minutes on the hour every hour beginning at nightfall, so plan to be in a spot where you can see it one evening. I defy you not to find this magical.

- If you want a picture of yourself or loved ones in front of the Eiffel Tower, it's not where you might think. The Eiffel Tower is located on the left bank in the seventh arrondissement in the Champ de Mars, but the classic shot with the Eiffel Tower in the background can be found on the right bank in the sixteenth arrondissement at the Place du Trocadéro.

- You can book a thirty-minute photo session with a professional English-speaking photographer at the Paris location of your choice on Flytographer.com, and you'll get all of the high-resolution digital images (without any extra charges) e-mailed to you within five days.

- Tip 10 percent in restaurants (cash only), and just leave one or two euros in more casual cafés. Know that there often isn't a line item for tips to be added to your credit-card bill, even in formal places, so be prepared with one- and two-euro coins. Round up for taxi drivers unless it's a longer fare from the airport, in which case tip as you see fit.

- If you are looking for simple ways to cut down on expenses during your trip, one easy way is to bypass the flat water or sparkling water question altogether and respond that you'd like *une carafe d'eau.* Substituting tap water for bottled water in cafés and brasseries can add up to significant savings if you are eating all of your meals out. In addition, the inexpensive house wine at French establishments is usually quite good, so don't feel the need to "order up" or get a bottle as you might back home. You can order a *pichet* of wine in various sizes if you're planning to have more than one glass.

- In Europe, prices at the counter are different from those at a table, so if you order a coffee while seated, it will be more expensive than if you stand at the bar and drink it.

- Even if you are traveling to France in the summertime, do not expect (or ask for) ice in your water or in other drinks. Some restaurants that cater to an international clientele do have it, but generally, ice water is just not a thing. If you have an open mind, you might find that water actually tastes so much better without the ice in it. Another bonus is the lack of condensation dripping all over everything.

- I am always amazed at the number of friends and acquaintances who ask me for recommendations for where to go in Paris in August. I've got one: don't go to Paris in August! I actually enjoy spending some time in Paris (or New York

City) in the summer because it's so quiet. Outside of the touristy areas, many neighborhoods in both cities are practically empty because almost all of the locals are gone. However, if you don't spend much time in Paris and you'd like to have a great Parisian vacation, August is not the time to go. Hardly any Parisians are there in August, so you're not getting a sense of the local culture because everyone around you will be either a tourist or someone catering to tourists. Almost every restaurant and store is closed for the entire month—and that is no exaggeration. There really isn't that much to do, and you'll be missing out on one of the main reasons to go to Paris, which is to watch the world go by and observe Parisians in their natural habitat. In addition, hardly any restaurants (or rental apartments) have air conditioning, which can get quite uncomfortable if it happens to be hot during your visit.

- Counting in France begins with thumbs, not pointer fingers, so use your thumb and pointer finger (instead of pointer and middle finger, which just means "peace") to signal to a waiter that you'd like a table for two people when asked, *vous êtes combien?*

- Take a few minutes to learn how to say *bonjour* and *au revoir* on YouTube, and use this to say hello and good-bye every time you enter and leave a restaurant, shop, or taxi. It doesn't matter if you're pronouncing it wrong, but it shows that you're making an effort and will make for a better experience.

- This took me a while to figure out, but compliment every French person who speaks English to you on how great his or her English is (even if it's not). Even the most hardened Parisian will soften up and then speak more English. It sounds silly, but it works nine times out of ten.

- Learning a little bit of French can be helpful, even if you don't currently have plans to travel to France. Spending just a few minutes per day on the language will help you when pronouncing fashion brand names, well-known artists, and French wines. Sign up for the free daily French pronunciation e-mails from Carrie Anne James of French is Beautiful; they're fun, helpful, and quick, taking only two minutes per day. If you want to go further with your French, you can do Carrie Anne's effective programs in the convenience of your home on your own schedule.

- Note that if you call a taxi via an app, phone, or your hotel concierge, the meter starts when the driver takes the job, so the meter is running before you even get in, which can get expensive. I recommend you take the subway, walk, or use Uber. Taxis can't pick up passengers near a designated taxi line, so head to the nearest line if you're having trouble hailing a cab. There are areas all over Paris, marked with a blue "TAXI" sign, and there should be available taxis lined up with green lights (red lights mean those cabs are unavailable). These designated areas are the modern-day version of Paris's *voitures de place* in the mid-1800s, though those obviously had horses instead of automobiles. There were 158 designated areas for carriages for hire to stand as they awaited customers.[72]

- Planning on doing some major shopping? Don't leave your hotel that day without your passport, because you will need it to fill out the necessary *détaxe* forms. Ask the sales associate to fill out the form for you and include a postage-paid envelope, and he or she will show you where to sign. Upon arrival at the airport when leaving France, go to the customs desk before checking in, and be prepared to show the merchandise that you bought, though this is rare. The customs officer will stamp your forms and show you where to mail them, usually at a nearby mailbox. Your refund will automatically be credited back to your card. Make sure to allow extra time at the airport for this (usually no more than thirty minutes at Charles de Gaulle and much less at smaller airports). If you've made some significant purchases in Paris, this is definitely worth the hassle.

- Here is a conversion method for clothing sizes, from US sizes to French ones: size 0 in the United States is a 34 in France; 2–4 is a 36; 4–6 is a 38; 8 is a 40; 10 is 42; 12 is 44; 14 is 46; 16 is 48; and so on. Shoes are a bit trickier. They sometimes go by French sizing but often go by Italian sizing because so many shoes are made in Italy, so don't assume anything. Try on multiple sizes to make sure you get the right fit. A 5.5 shoe size in the United States is a 37 in French sizing (36 in Italian); 6 is 37.5 in French sizing (36.5 in Italian); 6.5 is 38 in French (37 in Italian); 7 is 38.5 in French (37.5 in Italian); 7.5 is 39 in France (38 in Italian); 8 is 39.5 in French (38.5 in Italian); 8.5 is 40 in French (39 in Italian); 9 is 40.5 in French (39.5 in Italian); 9.5 is 41 in French (40 in Italian); 10 is 41.5 in French (40.5 in Italian); 10.5 is 42 in French (41 in Italian); 11 is 42.5 in French (41.5 in Italian).

- Sign up for the DoItInParis.com newsletter ahead of your trip. It lets you know the latest and greatest things to do in Paris, and it's available in both French and English. Or download the app. Also, check out the events calendar on SecretsofParis.com a few weeks prior to your trip and start planning.

- I'm sure you're already aware that many things are closed in Paris on Sundays, but this can be a real bummer if you're not mentally prepared for it (or even if you are). Residents learn to adjust and enjoy lazy Sundays, but this can prove tricky if you're a visitor looking for things to do. Many restaurants are also closed on Mondays and are often open only at specific times, so always do a quick Google search for everything before you head there to confirm *ouverture* and *fermeture*. Many museums are open on Sundays, as are most shops and restaurants in the Marais neighborhood.

- If you find yourself wandering around helplessly trying to find something open on a Sunday, a holiday, or any day in August, head to the Publicis Drugstore on Champs-Élysées. This street is the equivalent of Times Square in New York, and you generally should avoid it, but Publicis is an exception. Open every day until 2:00 a.m., it's a great spot to pick up everything from toiletries to chocolate to Champagne when most everything else is closed. You will never look at your local CVS or Duane Reade the same way again.

- Full-sized, full-powered hairdryers are a rarity in France. You could bring your own, but I've seen many a failure from friends bringing hairdryers, straighteners, and curling irons with US plugs to other countries, trying to make them work with adapters. Note that an adapter only changes the shape of a plug; it doesn't change the voltage. If it's really important to you to have these items with you, buy a converter or buy styling tools with universal voltage (available on Amazon, Sephora, or Net-a-Porter). But instead of going through all of that, I recommend you do as the Parisiennes do and work the low-maintenance hair look when in France. Think of it as a holiday for your hair.

- If you are going to an event, party, or dinner with friends or acquaintances while in Paris, be prepared for double kissing instead of handshakes and hugs. They are air kisses, so don't get too close, and lean to your left first and then to your right. This is done for all hellos and good-byes. It is time consuming, but once you get the hang of it, it is much less awkward than handshakes (which feel too stiff and formal) and hugs (which are way too intimate in certain cases).

- Practically everyone in France orders an espresso after a lunch or dinner, even if it's a decaf (*un déca*). It's a ritual, and it's a nice one. Take advantage of those long meals while you can. If you love sweets, the best coffee to order after a meal is a *café gourmand*, which is an espresso with a selection of the cutest mini desserts. This replaces the dessert course and allows you to taste several different treats without having to commit to just one.

- I cannot tell you the number of times in Paris that I've heard a Texan barrel into a restaurant asking for ice water *very loudly* or a New Yorker barrel into a store and start rattling off questions and demands *very loudly*. Though this can be embarrassing, turns out there is a legitimate reason for our "rude American" status. English is spoken from the diaphragm, so it is by nature much louder than French, which is spoken from the front of the mouth. There is a time and place for being loud and obnoxious (actually many times and many places, because it's just fun), but do know that it might be best to turn down the volume a few notches when traveling abroad. Unless you're going to, say, Oktoberfest.

To Do

There is so much to do in the most beautiful city in the world, but sometimes the best thing to do is nothing at all. Find a chair at Jardin des Tuileries or sit on a park bench in Place des Vosges, and watch the world go by. If you're more the restless type, pop on your headphones or grab the hand of a loved one, and just walk for hours. Observing the stunning architecture and fascinating people of Paris is free and highly entertaining. But in case you want some "real" things to do, here are some ideas:

- Enjoy whatever exhibition is on at the Grand Palais, and then cross the street to the Petit Palais. Escape the bustle of the street for a gorgeous courtyard setting, filled with mosaic floors, marbled columns, and a lush garden. It's the perfect stop for a rest, coffee, or restroom break.

- Book a wine-tasting class online before your trip with O Château (http://www.o-chateau.com/). The classes are taught in English, and the wine selection is always on point.

- Do not miss visiting the interior grounds of the Palais-Royal in the first arrondissement. Created in the seventeenth century by Cardinal Richelieu, it housed the royal families until Versailles was built. It later became a notorious spot for debauchery and prostitution, but today it's a serene space to eat, shop, stroll, and people-watch.

- Buy a bottle of Champagne and head to Île de la Cité and then down to the tip of the Square du Vert-Galant park. Watch the sun set over the Seine. Make out if you're with someone; enjoy the beautiful moment if you're alone.

- Head into the Four Seasons George V hotel and ogle the gorgeous flowers, even if you go just to use the restroom. If you're up for a splurge, grab a drink in the dark wood-paneled barroom and recap the day's events. It's a great way to spend a couple of hours. Nice hotel bars are kind of an obsession of mine, because you can sit and relax and enjoy the atmosphere and observe the other tourists plus some locals in their natural habitat. Really, who doesn't love a good hotel bar? Yes, they're expensive, but when on vacation, worth it. You can spend two euros getting a crappy espresso in some random place and feel ready to leave five minutes later, or you can spend ten euros at Le Meurice, getting an espresso that also comes with a couple of delicious chocolate bonbons or macarons; you'll never want to leave. It is an experience.

- Stroll through Jardin du Luxembourg, Jardin des Tuileries, and Place des Vosges. Repeat.

To Eat

Paris has so many places to eat that are really good; it almost seems pointless to make recommendations when you can just walk and explore and pop in somewhere that looks enticing. The one caveat is to avoid restaurants and cafés in touristy areas. Never ever eat at a place that has the menu posted in multiple languages out front. English menus offered once inside are different, and certainly helpful, but if they're posted with little American or British flags out front, move along to a street that feels less touristy. Outside of that, if you find a spot that's vibrant and full, you'd be hard-pressed to have a bad meal. I've listed below a few standbys that please everyone I recommend them to, but for a much more extensive list broken down by neighborhood, I suggest getting *Bright Lights Paris*, by Angie Niles, which is packed with great restaurant recommendations.

- Enjoy a scoop of Berthillon ice cream or sorbet on the Île Saint-Louis, and file under "touristy but wonderful." Instagram it immediately.

- Make lunch reservations at L'Oiseau Blanc at the Peninsula Paris. Yes, it's expensive, but the restaurant has the most insane view of the Eiffel Tower, and the food is classic and delicious. After lunch, head through the restaurant and pass the bar area to the long roof deck, where you can see all of Paris. I promise it's worth it. E-mailing for reservations doesn't work, so have your hotel concierge handle this one.

- Have lunch or dinner at Monsieur Bleu for the people-watching, delicious food, and divine interior architecture by Joseph Dirand. You can make reservations online on the restaurant's website. Check the Palais de Tokyo's website in advance, because Monsieur Bleu is located inside of it, and the Palais often has interesting art and cultural exhibitions.

- For a more classic (and more casual) Parisian dining experience, head to Bistrot Paul Bert in the eleventh arrondissement. The regularly rotating menu is filled with traditional, hearty, and extremely well-executed French dishes. Much has been written about Bistrot Paul Bert, so there will be other tourists, but it is completely authentic. Check the Instagram account @bistrotpaulbert if you're curious, because they usually take a snapshot of the daily specials.

- There is a restaurant in the eighth arrondissement where the interior is a bit cheesy (e.g., pictures of the owner posing with various French celebrities) and the lights are way too bright, but the food is just right. When I crave a classic Parisian meal, I head to Les Gourmets des Ternes. Everything is very simple but done just right and in a way that's becoming hard to find in Paris. The owners are there every night, and the menu rarely changes. To start, try the *fonds d'artichauts*, tomato salad, and leeks vinaigrette. As a main course, don't miss the "special" steak, served *à point*. Don't expect friendly servers, but do expect good food. Only go if you're in the mood for steak, and be sure to make reservations.

- Café de Flore is an institution for tourists and locals alike, sort of like Balthazar in New York. The food is kind of meh, but slowly savor a glass of Champagne there and you will understand its charms. You might end up sitting next to a French film celebrity such as Charlotte Rampling (who could easily be missed because of her general aloofness) or a French intellectual celebrity such as Bernard-Henri Lévy (not to be missed with his custom superdeep-V crisp white shirts), *or* you could end up sitting next to an annoying tourist asking for ice water very loudly in English. Every night at the Flore is a roulette! Whatever you do, don't insist that the salt-and-pepper potato chips served with the Champagne are so much better than those in the United States. They must fry them in some special oil, *non*? I insisted this for years until I saw bags and bags of potato chips rolled into the back of the restaurant one day, and they were…American. It just goes to show that atmosphere makes up for a lot.

- If you need a break from French food (or trying to order food in French), head to one of the Matsuri sushi restaurants. They have the rotating conveyor belts, which are associated with drunken college students and sake bombs in the States, but this is actually a decent sushi restaurant in Paris with a few locations. It's a good spot to go with kids (who like sushi). For even more options, head to Rue Saint-Anne in the first arrondissement for a variety of nonchain delicious and casual places for ramen, tonkatsu, udon, and dumplings. For the best Japanese desserts, matcha tea, and chirashi bowls, head to one of my favorite lunch spots in the world, Toraya at 10 rue Saint-Florentin in the first.

- If you're staying in a hotel, ask to have your minibar cleared out and stock up on items from your local Monoprix or

Monop. Food is one of the best reasons to travel to France, and starting your day with a typical Parisian breakfast in your room or packing a picnic for one of the glorious gardens is an inexpensive treat.

- If you're really into food and don't mind splurging on it, La Grande Epicerie inside of Le Bon Marché is the best grocery store in the world (in my opinion). If you're staying in Paris for one week or more, a visit to La Grande Epicerie is a must. It's not cheap, so buy your basics elsewhere, but it's a great place to buy high-quality olive oils, charcuterie, cheeses, wine, and specialty items from around the globe. Another similar option is the gourmet epicerie in the basement of the home store of Galeries Lafayette, though La Grande Epicerie is far better. Note that these are definitely not where local Parisians go because of the price point and general large-format ambiance (basically like an American grocery store except everything is of exceptional quality), but they are culinary heaven for tourists.

- Better yet, go to one of Paris's many *marchés* and enjoy the bounty of colorful produce, artisanal breads and cheeses, fresh fish, and locally made sausages, plus a plethora of personality. To me, this is one of the best parts about *la vie* in France. A day that begins with strolling through a market is a good one. Marché Raspail is the one near my Paris apartment, so of course I'm partial to it. Located on Boulevard Raspail in the sixth arrondissement near Le Bon Marché, it offers great food watching and people-watching, and it becomes an organic market on Sundays. The traditional market is open on Tuesday and Friday mornings, and the *biologique* market is on Sundays from 9:00 a.m. until 1:30 p.m., but know that some of the stalls will begin closing a bit before that. Another one of my favorites is Marché des Enfants Rouges. Located in the third arrondissement on Rue de Bretagne, it offers not only the usual roundup of excellent fresh French produce but also a fantastic Moroccan stall (warning: there's usually a long line). This market is a great experience for tourists and locals alike. It's also the oldest one in Paris. Make sure to save time for exploring around the market as well because there are great cheese shops and cafés to be found.

To Buy

There is much shopping to be had in Paris, which I'm sure you know because it's well documented. It's part of Paris's personality, really. There are entire Paris guides devoted just to shopping. I find that shopping is a highly personal thing because we all have different tastes and budgets, but below are a few things that I love that seem to be big hits with whomever I recommend them to.

- I believe that perfection can be found in France; it's hiding inside a Le Chocolat Alain Ducasse Manufacture à Paris boutique. You must try the *Tablette Mendiant 75% avec amandes, figues, et oranges confites*; it's a dark chocolate bar covered in whole caramelized almonds, pistachios, pine nuts, candied orange pieces, and morsels of figs that melt in your mouth. It blows my mind. Every time. And I've eaten a lot of them. There are full shops in the first, sixth, and eleventh arrondissements, plus it's available at Galeries Lafayette and the Eurostar boarding area at Gare du Nord. Buy some for yourself and some to bring back as gifts.

- In 1869, Aristide Boucicaut's Bon Marché in the left bank became the first store that was formally conceived and systematically designed to house a department store. In France, the United States, and the United Kingdom, the transition from small shop to department store occurred during the Industrial Revolution in the middle of the nineteenth century, and this one became a shopper's paradise for locals and tourists alike. It still is today, and it is hands down my favorite department store.

- For children's clothing and gifts that are chic and distinctly French, head to Bonton on Rue de Grenelle. For trendy children's items, head to Smallable Concept Store on Rue du Cherche-Midi.

- You can find linen napkins and bedding in a rainbow of colors at Merci on Boulevard Beaumarchais. They're easy to bring home, easy to wash, and nearly impossible to ruin. They strike the perfect balance between rustic and polished.

- It might just be my imagination, but I think that lavender oil (*huile essentielle de lavande*) is just better when you buy it in France. Bring some home and dab it on your neck and wrists at night, and dream of falling asleep in a field of lavender in Provence.

- Make sure to save time to do a little vintage and antique shopping. My absolute best vintage fashion and antique furniture finds have been from Paris. A *dépôt-vente* is the name for consignment shop in French.

- It doesn't get any better than the world-famous flea market called Marché aux Puces located in a slightly dodgy but up-and-coming area on the outskirts of Paris called Saint-Ouen. The closest station is Porte de Clignancourt at the end of the four line. Once off the subway, hold on to your handbag, and don't make eye contact with anyone until you pass the street stalls and get into the official market. People will try to sell you fake handbags and other counterfeit items. If it's your first time, look for the signs leading to the Paul Bert, which is a good starting point. Though these mostly contain antique furniture, there are several different shops within the Marché aux Puces that offer vintage fashion at all different price points. Plan to spend the day, and be prepared with cash because not all vendors accept credit cards, and don't be afraid to negotiate. The market is open to the public every Saturday, Sunday, and Monday. Maison Food Market, found at 77 rue des Rosiers, offers good casual food and a boho Brooklyn-ish atmosphere.

- If high-end vintage clothing and accessories are your thing, make sure to visit Les Trois Marchés de Catherine B in the sixth arrondissement, which specializes in Chanel and Hermès. Meanwhile, over on the right bank, you will find a very famous vintage shop, Didier Ludot, located in the Palais-Royal. It is full of the most fantastic luxe vintage treasures you can imagine, but be prepared for some major attitude with prices to match. This is not a fun place to "just browse," but if you're serious and ready to splurge, you will find pristine-condition 1960s Balenciaga, Christian Dior, and more. For a still-high-end-but-much-friendlier shopping experience, head a few doors over to Gabrielle Geppert.

- If Paris fashion and New York fashion had a baby, it would be Montaigne Market. Located on Avenue Montaigne in the eighth arrondissement, this multibrand luxury clothing and accessories store has all-black monotone looks in the front to please the Parisiennes and fun stuff in the back to please everyone else. It is a luxury store with luxury prices, but if you're up for a splurge or an afternoon of window shopping, this is the place to do it.

- Though this one is written up in every guide to Paris, I must include it: Colette. This right bank concept store is still a good place to go if you need to buy gifts because the main floor offers all kinds of cool books and tchotchkes. The Water Bar downstairs is a nice place to go for a casual-but-chic lunch.

- In the United States, I'm passionate about supporting local and small businesses. Whether it's food or fashion, I aim to be purposeful with my spending and shop sustainably. Chain stores and restaurants do not appeal to me at all, for a variety of concerns, including labor conditions, environmental impacts, and lack of authenticity. I try to buy things that create good situations for everyone involved, from the manufacturers to the suppliers to the retailers to me. I believe we should applaud companies that are trying to improve their business practices and support them with our spending power. However, I have a soft spot for chain stores when I travel abroad. I drop my activist attitude and just enjoy. In the face of linguistic challenges, mass-market stores can be comforting, and visiting a chain shop or restaurant can provide another way to understand a country's popular culture. That was my long-winded intro to my love for the chain store Monoprix. It is sort of like a smaller version of Target because it sells food, housewares, clothing, and various supplies, but it is so much better. If you're renting an apartment in Paris, you can make one stop to the Monoprix and find everything you need for your stay. The quality of the food in France is light years ahead of America, and chain grocery stores are no exception. It would be much better to shop for cheese at a neighborhood *fromagerie* and pop into a *pharmacie* to pick up the toiletries you need for your stay, but there's something to be said about landing in France and getting all of your necessities in one place. "Necessary" is, of course, a relative term, and here are some of mine:

- Diadermine Expert Rides 3D Patchs Anti-Rides Haute Performance eye patches. These things are awesome. I am never without a box because I buy a ton every time I go to France. They're far more effective than anything I've found in the United States, and they're a fraction of the price. Puffy eyes? Hungover? Accidentally slept on your side and got smashy creased eyes? These eye patches will help in ten minutes flat.

- Head to the yogurt section and get Gervita and Perle de Lait in the plain "nature" flavor. As long as you're used to eating plain or Greek yogurt and fromage blanc, you'll love this. Buy some honey and fruit as toppings and enjoy.

- The single-serve lettuce packs are just perfect for storing in a hotel minibar or for buying for a picnic. My favorite kind is the mâche, which tastes delicious with ham, cheese, avocado, olive oil, salt, pepper, and Dijon, whether served as a salad or as a sandwich on a baguette.

- I never thought I would get excited about water, but I'm obsessed with one called Contrex, which can be found at every Monoprix. It is apparently extra high in calcium and magnesium, it helps with digestion, and it has a delicious taste that's almost milky. It's also totally acceptable to rip into a six-pack of bottled water and take out just one to put by your bedside table, so don't feel like you have to buy (and carry) all six.

- For macarons, I love Pierre Hermé. Yes, it is an international chain, so you're not going to have an artisanal experience, but it is the place to go if you like adventurous macaron flavors. It would be a shame to go here and get basic flavors like *framboise, chocolat, et vanille* when you can have flavor combinations like fig with foie gras and white truffles with hazelnuts. While other macarons are often uniform throughout, the exteriors of these macarons crackle like eggshells into the thick gooey ganache, which is light and pillowy soft. If you see the salted dark chocolate bar called *tablette de chocolat noir*, grab one (or five) and thank me later.

Acknowledgments

First of all, I must thank Paris for being an endless source of inspiration. It is the most beautiful city in the world, and its charms have been casting spells on visitors for centuries. Its magic bowled me over upon my first arrival, and it continues to mystify and enchant me to this day.

There are not enough ways to say *merci* to express just how much I appreciate my wonderful husband, Jason, for his love, friendship, and oodles of support. My darling daughter, Sloane, *ma petite* Francophone extraordinaire, is turning into an impressive little lady who inspires me daily. It pleases me to no end to watch her grow up. These two are the ultimate companions for adventures in France and in life.

Through all of my friends—Americans, French, and faux French alike—I've learned how to make the transition in life from a dazed and confused young mother to a much more confident and worldly adult. So thank you, my friends, for being your wonderful selves and for teaching me so much. In my friend Carrie Anne James, I finally found someone who is as obsessed with Paris as I am. She has been a tremendous help in my journey of learning the French language, and she is the one person I can talk to about Paris who just gets it.

It is hard to explain just how important the Lycée Français de New York has become to my family. At first, I thought it was just a school—and an intimidating one at that—but it turned out to be so much more. After-school pickup during the first year was frankly a bit terrifying because, as I've covered in detail in this book, French women can be a bit difficult to get to know. My daughter immediately loved it because daily life there is never dull. With children from more than fifty nationalities, it is a truly wonderful institution that is preparing my daughter to be a citizen of the world. All of the push and pull that I've described in this book between French and American cultures is not an issue at LFNY, which expertly blends the best aspects from both cultures. As for me, I've met some of my closest friends through the school and now cannot imagine life without my lovely Lycée mommies. It is a special group.

But before feeling like we fit in at LFNY, my husband and I were happily greeted at the French Institute Alliance Française (FIAF). We had just moved back to the United States from Paris and were first-time residents of New York. We were no longer Californians, not yet true New Yorkers, and definitely not French, so we felt like we were in limbo. The kind and generous FIAF family welcomed us warmly from the beginning. It is not just a language and cultural center; it's a community that helps provide a sense of belonging for French expats and Francophiles alike. Marie-Monique Steckel is a perfect example of the greatness that happens when one combines American warmth, openness, and ideas with French candor and the courage to be daring.

And finally, thank you to the writers whose words I found especially helpful: Olivier Magny, Joan DeJean, and Sudhir Hazareesingh.

About the Author

Jordan Phillips holds a master's degree in fashion marketing and management from the École Supérieure des Arts et Techniques de la Mode (ESMOD) in Paris, and a bachelor's degree in journalism from California Polytechnic State University, San Luis Obispo (Cal Poly). She is the founder of Lure of Luxe LLC.

She is also the author of *Sustainable Luxe: A Guide to Feel-Good Fashion* and *The Lure of Luxe: Climbing the Luxury Consumption Pyramid.*

She currently lives in New York City with her husband and daughter and visits her apartment in Paris as often as possible.

For more information, please visit www.inspiredbyparis.com.

Sources

Adams, Trevor. "The Essay: Stars in Stripes." *The Independent,* July 10, 1999.

Baxter, John. *Five Nights in Paris: After Dark in the City of Light.* New York: Harper Perennial, 2015.

BCG Report, *Navigating the New Consumer Realities: Consumer Sentiment 2011.* The Boston Consulting Group, June 2011.

Berest, Anne, Audrey Diwan, Caroline de Maigret, and Sophie Mas. *How to Be Parisian Wherever You Are: Love, Style, and Bad Habits.* New York: Doubleday, 2014.

Betts, Kate. *My Paris Dream: An Education in Style, Slang, and Seduction in the Great City on the Seine.* New York: Spiegel & Grau, 2015.

Burke, Carolyn. *No Regrets: The Life of Edith Piaf.* Chicago: Alfred A. Knopf, 2011.

Chevalier, Jim. *About the Baguette: Exploring the Origin of a French National Icon.* Chez Jim Books, 2012.

Collins, Lauren. "Bread Winner." *The New Yorker,* December 3, 2012.

Davies, Lucia. "Paris." *AnOther Magazine,* May 31, 2011. Accessed December 21, 2015. http://www.anothermag.com/art-photography/1122/paris.

DeJean, Joan. *The Essence of Style: How the French Invented High Fashion, Fine Food, Chic Cafes, Style, Sophistication, and Glamour.* New York: Free Press, 2005.

DeJean, Joan. *How Paris Became Paris: The Invention of the Modern City.* New York: Bloomsbury, 2014.

Druckerman, Pamela. "France's Cult of Fearlessness." *New York Times,* November 27, 2015.

Fagan, Chelsea. "Paris Syndrome: A First-Class Problem for a First-Class Vacation." *The Atlantic,* October 18, 2011. Accessed September 22, 2015. http://www.theatlantic.com/health/archive/2011/10/paris-syndrome-a-first-class-problem-for-a-first-class-vacation/246743/.

Garelick, Rhonda K. *Mademoiselle: Coco Chanel and the Pulse of History.* New York: Random House, 2014.

Goodreads. "Angela Carter (Quotes)." Accessed September 25, 2015.

Gunn, Tim. *A Guide to Quality, Taste & Style.* New York: Abrams Image, 2007.

Hazareesingh, Sudhir. *How the French Think: An Affectionate Portrait of an Intelligent People.* New York: Basic Books, 2015.

Hemphill, C. Scott, and Jeannie Suk. "The Law, Culture, and Economics of Fashion." *Stanford Law Review* (2009).

History.com. "Eiffel Tower." Accessed November 10, 2015. http://www.history.com/topics/eiffel-tower.

"INSEE: Les Français gagnent en moyenne 2 202 euros nets par mois." *Le Parisien*, September 16, 2015.

Joynt, Carol Ross. "How a French Diplomat Crisis Involving Javier Bardem Could Impact Washington." *Washingtonian*, February 26, 2014. Accessed December 15, 2015. http://www.washingtonian.com/blogs/capitalcomment/local-news/how-a-french-diplo-matic-crisis-involving-javier-bardem-could-impact-washington.php.

Kapferer, Jean-Noel, and Vincent Bastien. *The Luxury Strategy*. London: Kogan Page, 2009.

Khorosh, Marina. "French Girls Don't Do It Better: One Writer on Her Return to New York." *Vogue*, October 29, 2015. Accessed October 30, 2015. http://www.vogue.com/13364220/parisian-style-vs-new-york-style/?mbid=nl_102915_Daily&CNDID=31421658&spMailin gID=12376935&spUserID=ODY5NDgzNzY2MzAS1&spJobID=603 852090&spReportId=NjAzODUyMDkwS0.

Kirkland, Stephane. *Paris Reborn: Napoleon III, Baron Haussmann, and the Quest to Build a Modern City*. New York: St. Martin's Press, 2013.

Lewis, Danny. *Brigitte Bardot: Liberte*. Amazon Digital Services, 2014.

Magny, Olivier. *Into Wine: An Invitation to Pleasure*. New Orleans: Gourmand Horizons, 2013.

Magny, Olivier. *Stuff Parisians Like: Discovering the Quoi in the Je Ne Sais Quoi*. New York: The Berkley Publishing Group, 2011.

Mah, Ann. *Mastering the Art of French Eating: From Paris Bistros to Farmhouse Kitchens, Lessons in Food and Love*. New York: Penguin Group, 2013.

Musée d'Orsay, Paris. "Splendeurs et miseres: images de la prostitution 1850–1910." Visited November 10, 2015.

Nossiter, Adam, and Rick Gladstone. "Paris Attacks Kill More Than 100, Police Say; Border Controls Tightened." *New York Times*, November 13, 2015. Accessed November 14, 2015. http://www.nytimes.com/2015/11/14/world/europe/paris-shooting-attacks.html?smid=tw-share#permid=16662404.

Phillips, Lynn. "Crossing the Line." *T Magazine*, April 14, 2011.

Plummer, Robert. "Do Americans Dream of Longer Holidays?" *BBC News*, November 4, 2015. Accessed November 4, 2015. http://www.bbc.com/news/business-34714064?ocid=socialflow_twitter.

Redman, Laura Dannen. "Why Are Americans So Afraid of Vacation?" *Condé Nast Traveler*, December 21, 2015. Accessed December 24, 2015. http://www.cntraveler.com/stories/2015-12-21/why-are-americans-so-afraid-of-vacation?mbid=social_twitter.

Rosenbloom, Stephanie. "What a Great Trip! And I'm Not Even There Yet." *New York Times*, May 7, 2014.

Rounding, Virginia. *Grandes Horizontales: The Lives and Legends of Four Nineteenth-Century Courtesans.* London: Bloomsbury, 2003.

Sciolino, Elaine. *La Seduction: How the French Play the Game of Life.* New York: Times Books, 2011.

Sciolino, Elaine. *The Only Street in Paris: Life on the Rue des Martyrs.* New York: W. W. Norton & Company, 2015.

Sciolino, Elaine. "Paris, One Step at a Time." *New York Times*, October 4, 2015.

Seward, Desmond. *Eugénie: The Empress and Her Empire.* London: Thistle Publishing, 2013.

Seward, Desmond. *Marie Antoinette.* London: Thistle Publishing, 2015.

Smith, Ray A. "The Clothes Seemed Great in the Store: Why People Regularly Wear Just 20% of Their Wardrobe." *Wall Street Journal,* April 18, 2013.

Smithsonian.com. "Is the Croissant Really French?" Amanda Fiegl, April 30, 2015. Accessed December 23, 2015. http://www.smithsonianmag.com/travel/croissant-really-french-180955130/.

Smithsonian.com. "When Food Changed History: The French Revolution." Lisa Bramen. July 14, 2010. Accessed December 23, 2015. http://www.smithsonianmag.com/arts-culture/when-food-changed-history-the-french-revolution-93598442/?no-ist.

Sozzani, Franca, "Editor's Blog." *Vogue Italia.* December 28, 2010. Accessed September 22, 2015. http://www.vogue.it/en/magazine/editor-s-blog/2010/12/december-28th#ad-image54901.

Stimmler-Hall, Heather. *Naughty Paris: A Lady's Guide to the Sexy City.* Paris: Fleur de Lire Press, 2015.

Tartetatin.org. "History of the Tarte Tatin." Accessed December 21, 2015. http://www.tartetatin.org/home/history-of-the-tarte-tatin.

Thurman, Judith. *Secrets of the Flesh: A Life of Colette.* New York: The Ballatine Publishing Group, 1999.

TourEiffel.paris. "Painting the Eiffel Tower." Accessed December 7, 2015. http://www.toureiffel.paris/en/everything-about-the-tower/themed-files/97.html.

TradingEconomics.com. "France Youth Unemployment Rate." Accessed October 31, 2015. http://www.tradingeconomics.com/france/youth-unemployment-rate.

Weinraub, Judith. "The Fall and Rise of French Bread." *The Washington Post*, August 24, 2005. Accessed December 23, 2015. http://www.washingtonpost.com/wp-dyn/content/article/2005/08/23/AR2005082300291.html.

Wikifashion.com "Breton Stripes." Accessed January 17, 2015. http://wikifashion.com/wiki/Breton_stripes.

Wood, Ean. *The Josephine Baker Story*. London: Omnibus Press, 2010.

Wyatt, Caroline. "'Paris Syndrome' Strikes Japanese." *BBC News*, December 20, 2006. Accessed September 22, 2015. http://news.bbc.co.uk/go/pr/fr/-/2/hi/europe/6197921.stm.

Index

Endnotes

1   Stephanie Rosenbloom, "What a Great Trip! And I'm Not Even There Yet," *New York Times*, May 7, 2014.

2   "Angela Carter (Quotes)," Goodreads, accessed September 25, 2015, http://www.goodreads.com/quotes/335167-anticipation-is-the-greater-part-of-pleasure.

3   Marina Khorosh, "French Girls Don't Do It Better: One Writer on Her Return to New York," *Vogue*, October 29, 2015, accessed October 30, 2015, http://www.vogue.com/13364220/parisian-style-vs-new-york-style/?mbid=nl_102915_Daily&CNDID=31421658&spMailingID=12376935&spUserID=ODY5NDgzNzY2MzAS1&spJobID=603852090&spReportId=NjAzODUyMDkwS0.

4   Olivier Magny, *Stuff Parisians Like: Discovering the Quoi in the Je Ne Sais Quoi* (New York: The Berkley Publishing Group, 2011).

5   Joan DeJean, *The Essence of Style: How the French Invented High Fashion, Fine Food, Chic Cafes, Style, Sophistication, and Glamour* (New York: Free Press, 2005).

6   Ibid.

7   BCG Report, *Navigating the New Consumer Realities: Consumer Sentiment 2011* (The Boston Consulting Group, June 2011).

8   Joan DeJean, *The Essence of Style: How the French Invented High Fashion, Fine Food, Chic Cafes, Style, Sophistication, and Glamour* (New York: Free Press, 2005).

9   Joan DeJean, *How Paris Became Paris: The Invention of the Modern City* (New York: Bloomsbury, 2014).

10 Stephane Kirkland, *Paris Reborn: Napoléon III, Baron Haussmann, and the Quest to Build a Modern City* (New York: St. Martin's Press, 2013).

11 Joan DeJean, *The Essence of Style: How the French Invented High Fashion, Fine Food, Chic Cafes, Style, Sophistication, and Glamour* (New York: Free Press, 2005).

12 "Eiffel Tower," History.com, accessed November 10, 2015, http://www.history.com/topics/eiffel-tower.

13 Ibid.

14 "Painting the Eiffel Tower," TourEiffel.paris, accessed December 7, 2015, http://www.toureiffel.paris/en/everything-about-the-tower/themed-files/97.html.

15 Robert Plummer, "Do Americans Dream of Longer Holidays?" *BBC News*, November 4, 2015, http://www.bbc.com/news/business-34714064?ocid=socialflow_twitter.

16 Laura Dannen Redman, "Why Are Americans So Afraid of Vacation?" *Condé Nast Traveler*, December 21, 2015, accessed December 24, 2015, http://www.cntraveler.com/stories/2015-12-21/why-are-americans-so-afraid-of-vacation?mbid=social_twitter.

17 Carol Ross Joynt, "How a French Diplomat Crisis Involving Javier Bardem Could Impact Washington," *Washingtonian*, February 26, 2014, accessed December 15, 2015, http://www.washingtonian.com/blogs/capitalcomment/local-news/

how-a-french-diplomatic-crisis-involving-javier-bardem-could-impact-washington.php.

[18] Heather Stimmler-Hall, *Naughty Paris: A Lady's Guide to the Sexy City* (Paris: Fleur de Lire Press, 2015).

[19] Musee d'Orsay, Paris, "Splendeurs et miseres: images de la prostitution 1850–1910." Visited November 10, 2015.

[20] Virginia Rounding, *Grandes Horizontales: The Lives and Legends of Four Nineteenth-Century Courtesans* (London: Bloomsbury, 2003).

[21] Anne Berest, Audrey Diwan, Caroline de Maigret, and Sophie Mas, *How to Be Parisian Wherever You Are: Love, Style, and Bad Habits* (New York: Doubleday, 2014).

[22] "INSEE: Les Français gagnent en moyenne 2 202 euros nets par mois," *Le Parisien*, September 16, 2015.

[23] "France Youth Unemployment Rate," TradingEconomics.com, accessed October 31, 2015, http://www.tradingeconomics.com/france/youth-unemployment-rate.

[24] Caroline Wyatt, "'Paris Syndrome' Strikes Japanese," *BBC News*, December 20, 2006, accessed September 22, 2015, http://news.bbc.co.uk/go/pr/fr/-/2/hi/europe/6197921.stm.

[25] Chelsea Fagan, "Paris Syndrome: A First-Class Problem for a First-Class Vacation," *The Atlantic*, October 18, 2011, accessed September 22, 2015, http://www.theatlantic.com/health/archive/2011/10/paris-syndrome-a-first-class-problem-for-a-first-class-vacation/246743/.

[26] Elaine Sciolino, "Paris, One Step at a Time," *New York Times*, October 4, 2015.

[27] Joan DeJean, *How Paris Became Paris: The Invention of the Modern City* (New York: Bloomsbury, 2014).

[28] Elaine Sciolino, *La Seduction: How the French Play the Game of Life* . (New York: Times Books, 2011).

29   Joan DeJean, *The Essence of Style: How the French Invented High Fashion, Fine Food, Chic Cafes, Style, Sophistication, and Glamour* (New York: Free Press, 2005).

30   Elaine Sciolino, *La Seduction: How the French Play the Game of Life* (New York: Times Books, 2011).

31   Joan DeJean, *The Essence of Style: How the French Invented High Fashion, Fine Food, Chic Cafes, Style, Sophistication, and Glamour* (New York: Free Press, 2005).

32   "When Food Changed History: The French Revolution," Lisa Bremen, Smithsonian.com, July 14, 2010, accessed December 23, 2015, http://www.smithsonianmag.com/arts-culture/when-food-changed-history-the-french-revolution-93598442/?no-ist.

33   "Is the Croissant Really French?" Amanda Fiegl, Smithsonian.com, April 30, 2015, Accessed December 23, 2015, http://www.smithsonianmag.com/travel/croissant-really-french-180955130/.

34   Judith Weinraub, "The Fall and Rise of French Bread," *The Washington Post*, August 24, 2005, accessed December 23, 2015, http://www.washingtonpost.com/wp-dyn/content/article/2005/08/23/AR2005082300291.html.

35   Lauren Collins, "Bread Winner," *The New Yorker*, December 3, 2012.

36   Ann Mah, *Mastering the Art of French Eating: From Paris Bistros to Farmhouse Kitchens, Lessons in Food and Love* (New York: Penguin Group, 2013).

37   John Baxter, *Five Nights in Paris: After Dark in the City of Light* (New York: Harper Perennial, 2015).

38   Ann Mah, *Mastering the Art of French Eating: From Paris Bistros to Farmhouse Kitchens, Lessons in Food and Love* (New York: Penguin Group, 2013).

39   "History of the Tarte Tatin," Tartetatin.org, accessed December 21, 2015, http://www.tartetatin.org/home/history-of-the-tarte-tatin.

40 Joan DeJean, *The Essence of Style: How the French Invented High Fashion, Fine Food, Chic Cafes, Style, Sophistication, and Glamour* (New York: Free Press, 2005).

41 Olivier Magny, *Into Wine: An Invitation to Pleasure* (New Orleans: Gourmand Horizons, 2013).

42 Ibid.

43 Blackpoodles, November 13, 2015, comment on Adam Nossiter and Rick Gladstone, "Paris Attacks Kill More Than 100, Police Say; Border Controls Tightened," *New York Times*, November 13, 2015, accessed November 14, 2015, http://www.nytimes.com/2015/11/14/world/europe/paris-shooting-attacks.html?smid=tw-share#permid=16662404.

44 Sudhir Hazareesingh, *How the French Think: An Affectionate Portrait of an Intelligent People* (New York: Basic Books, 2015).

45 Pamela Druckerman, "France's Cult of Fearlessness," *New York Times*, November 27, 2015.

46 Jean-Noel Kapferer and Vincent Bastien, *The Luxury Strategy* (London: Kogan Page, 2009).

47 Stephane Kirkland, *Paris Reborn: Napoléon III, Baron Haussmann, and the Quest to Build a Modern City* (New York: St. Martin's Press, 2013).

48 C. Scott Hemphill and Jeannie Suk, "The Law, Culture, and Economics of Fashion," *Stanford Law Review* (2009).

49 Ibid.

50 Ray A. Smith, "The Clothes Seemed Great in the Store: Why People Regularly Wear Just 20% of Their Wardrobe," *Wall Street Journal*, April 18, 2013.

51 Lynn Phillips, "Crossing the Line," *T Magazine*, April 14, 2011.

52 Trevor Adams, "The Essay: Stars in Stripes," *The Independent*, July 10, 1999.

53 Franca Sozzani, "Editor's Blog," *Vogue Italia*, published December 28, 2010, http://www.vogue.it/en/magazine/editor-s-blog/2010/12/december-28th#ad-image54901.

54 Tim Gunn, *A Guide to Quality, Taste & Style* (New York: Abrams Image, 2007).

55 Danny Lewis, *Brigitte Bardot: Liberte* (Amazon Digital Services, 2014).

56 Rhonda K. Garelick, *Mademoiselle: Coco Chanel and the Pulse of History* (New York: Random House, 2014).

57 Carolyn Burke, *No Regrets: The Life of Edith Piaf* (Chicago: Alfred A. Knopf, 2011).

58 Ean Wood, *The Josephine Baker Story* (London: Omnibus Press, 2010).

59 Ibid.

60 Ibid.

61 Desmond Seward, *Marie Antoinette* (London: Thistle Publishing, 2015).

62 Ibid.

63 Ibid.

64 Kate Betts, *My Paris Dream: An Education in Style, Slang, and Seduction in the Great City on the Seine* (New York: Spiegel & Grau, 2015).

65 John Baxter, *Five Nights in Paris: After Dark in the City of Light* (New York: Harper Perennial, 2015).

66 Elaine Sciolino, *The Only Street in Paris: Life on the Rue des Martyrs* (New York: W. W. Norton & Company, 2015).

67 Joan DeJean, *The Essence of Style: How the French Invented High Fashion, Fine Food, Chic Cafes, Style, Sophistication, and Glamour* (New York: Free Press, 2005).

68 Joan DeJean, *How Paris Became Paris: The Invention of the Modern City* (New York: Bloomsbury, 2014).

69 Ibid.

70 Ibid.

71   John Baxter, *Five Nights in Paris: After Dark in the City of Light* (New York: Harper Perennial, 2015).

72   Stephane Kirkland, *Paris Reborn: Napoleon III, Baron Haussmann, and the Quest to Build a Modern City* (New York: St. Martin's Press, 2013).

Made in the USA
San Bernardino, CA
21 December 2017